Foreword

Life is about experience and travel will for all intent and purpose bestow you a greater perspective on life and of course many experiences which will accompany you through the many paths this life will take.

Paul has in this publication shared with you the reader a sample of his life within the hectic lifestyle of a Television personality, a sample of photos taken around the world which presented in such a unique way for your pleasure.

The book is also dedicated to his family in a way to thank them both for their patience and their continued love which I hear him mention often.

It has been a pleasure to work with Paul during our travels and as we continue to work and climb through haunted castles and tunnels his collection of memories will increase vastly along with the photographs.

- Barry Fitzgerald.

IRELAND IRELAND

postcard

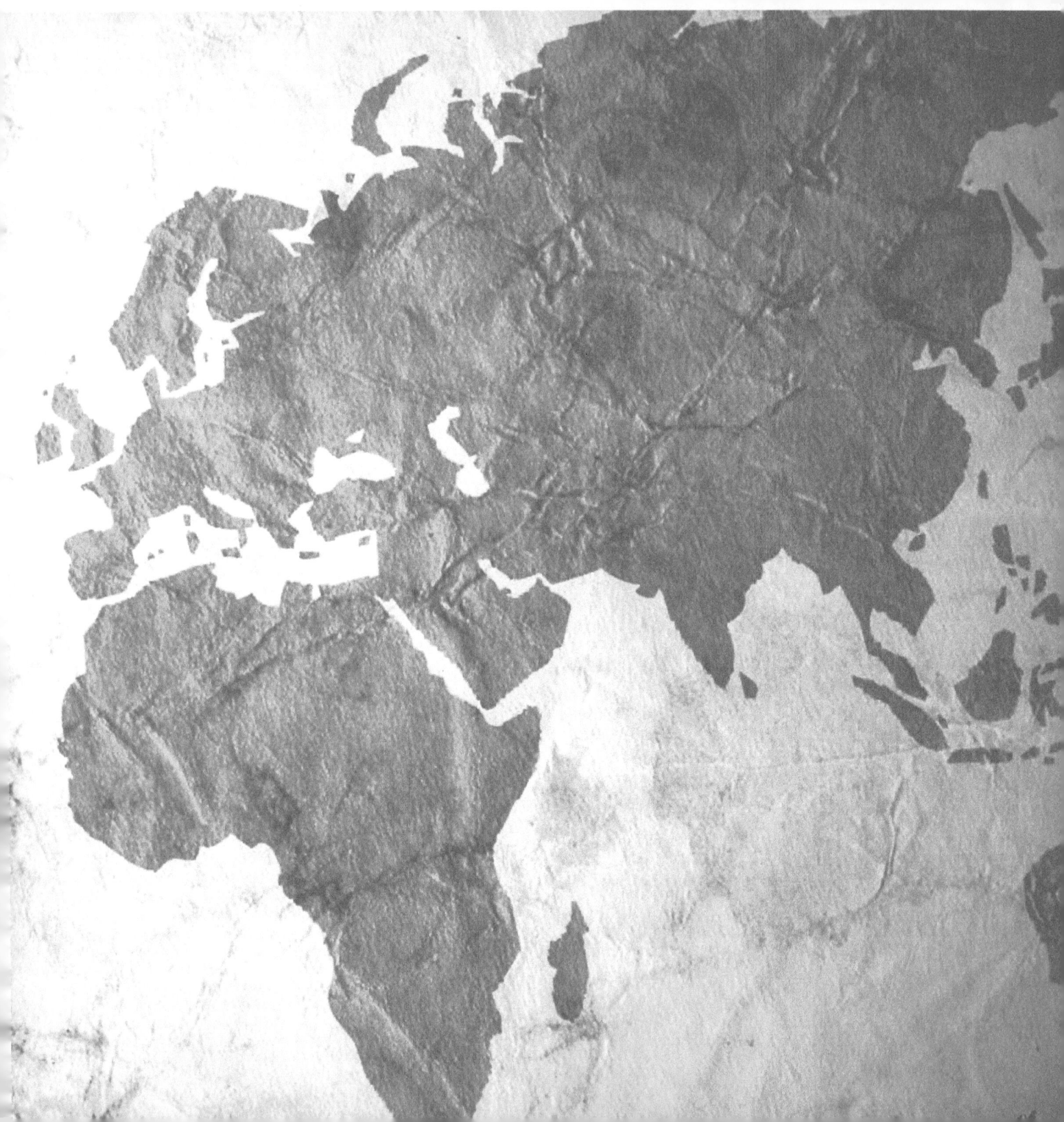

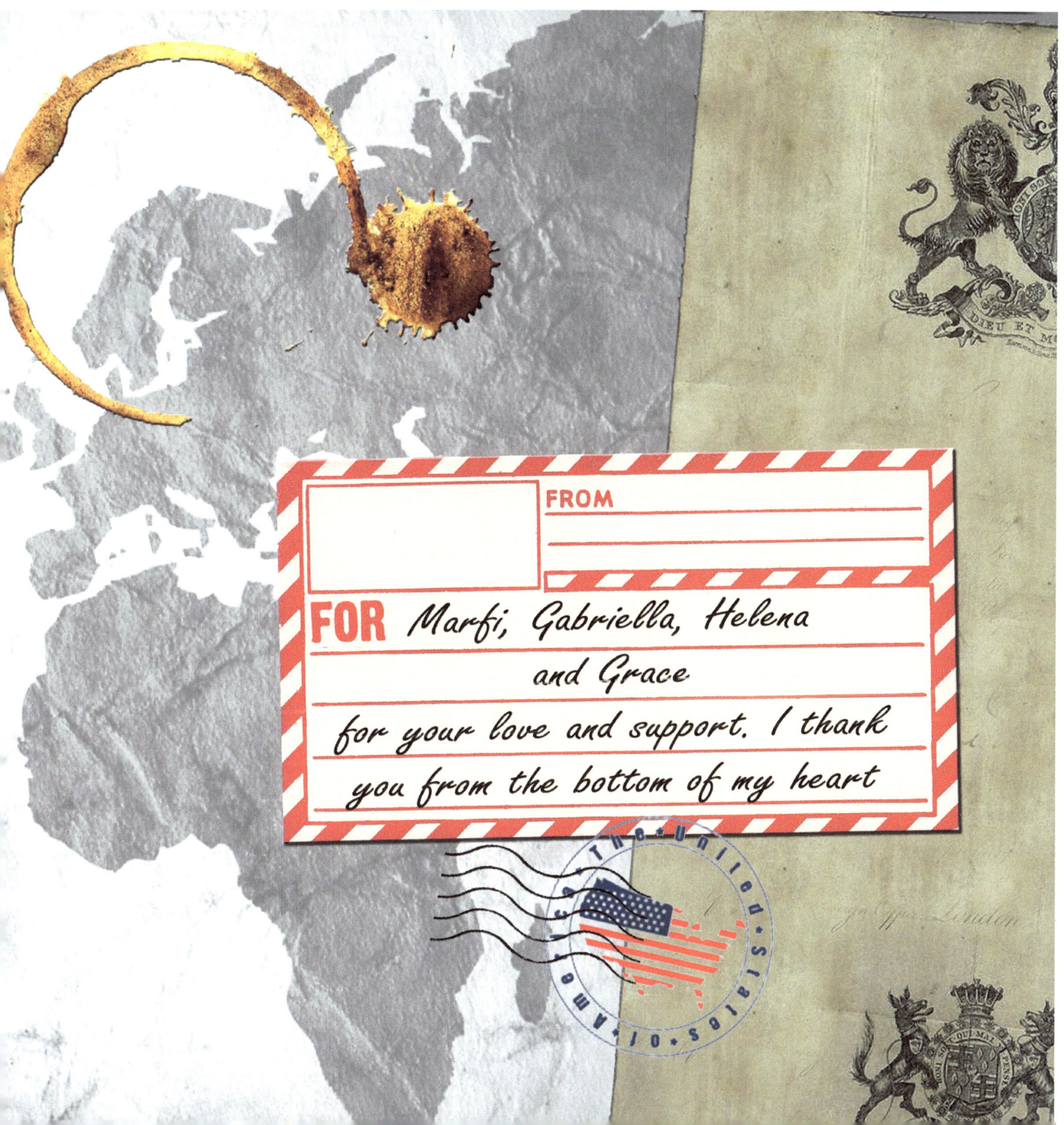

FROM

FOR Marfi, Gabriella, Helena
and Grace

for your love and support. I thank
you from the bottom of my heart

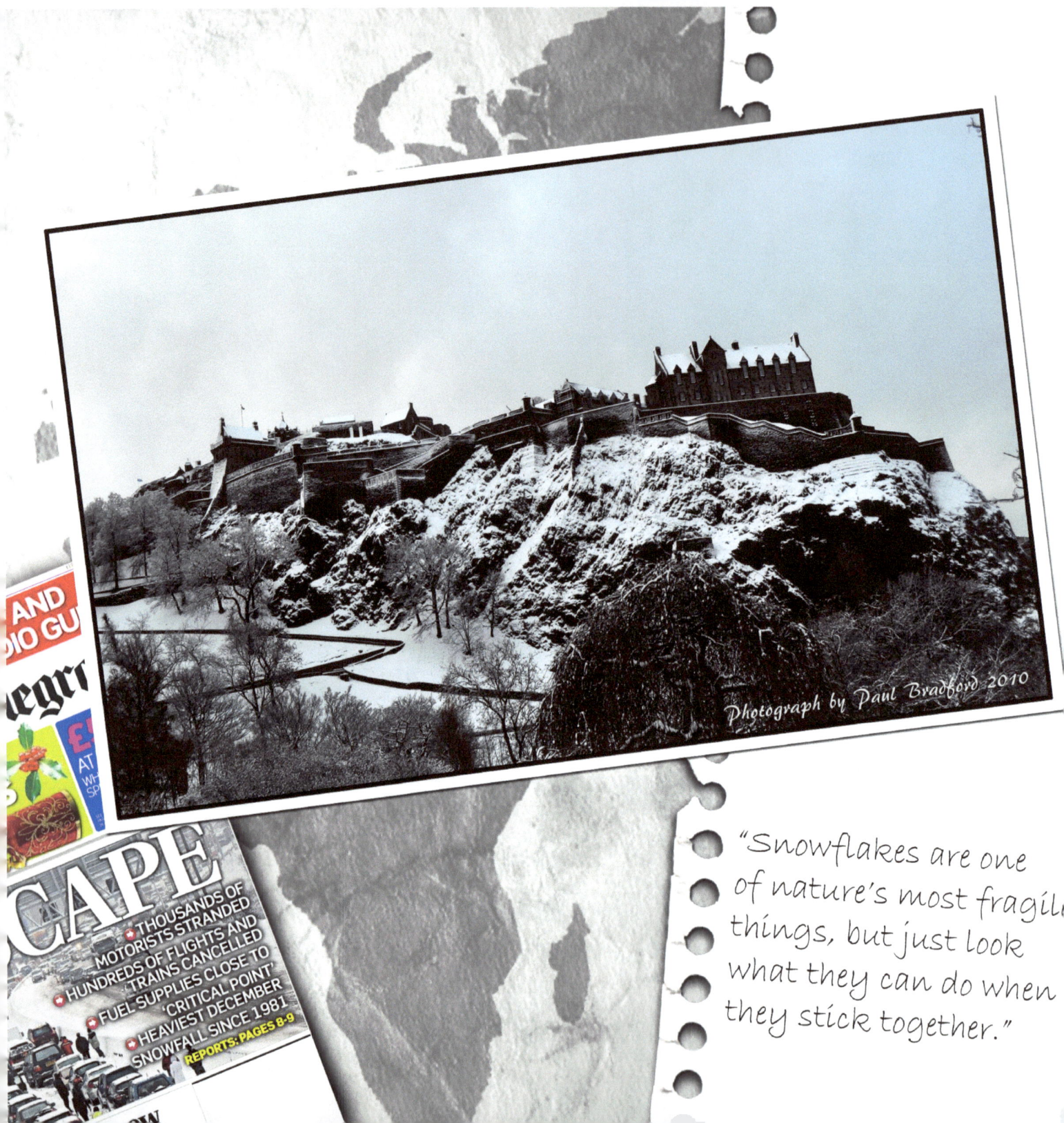

Photograph by Paul Bradford 2010

"Snowflakes are one of nature's most fragile things, but just look what they can do when they stick together."

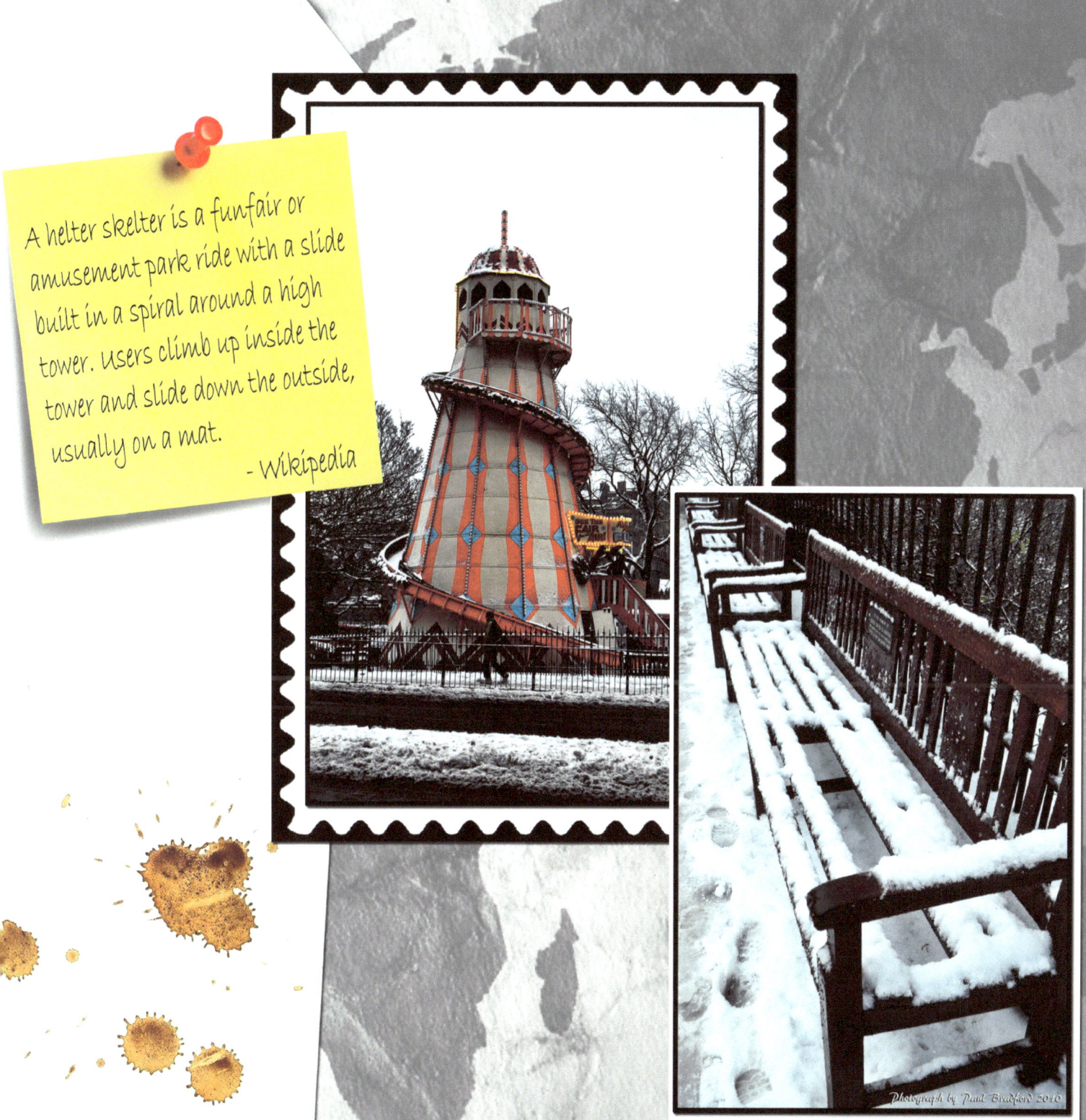

A helter skelter is a funfair or amusement park ride with a slide built in a spiral around a high tower. Users climb up inside the tower and slide down the outside, usually on a mat.

- Wikipedia

Photograph by Paul Bradford 2010

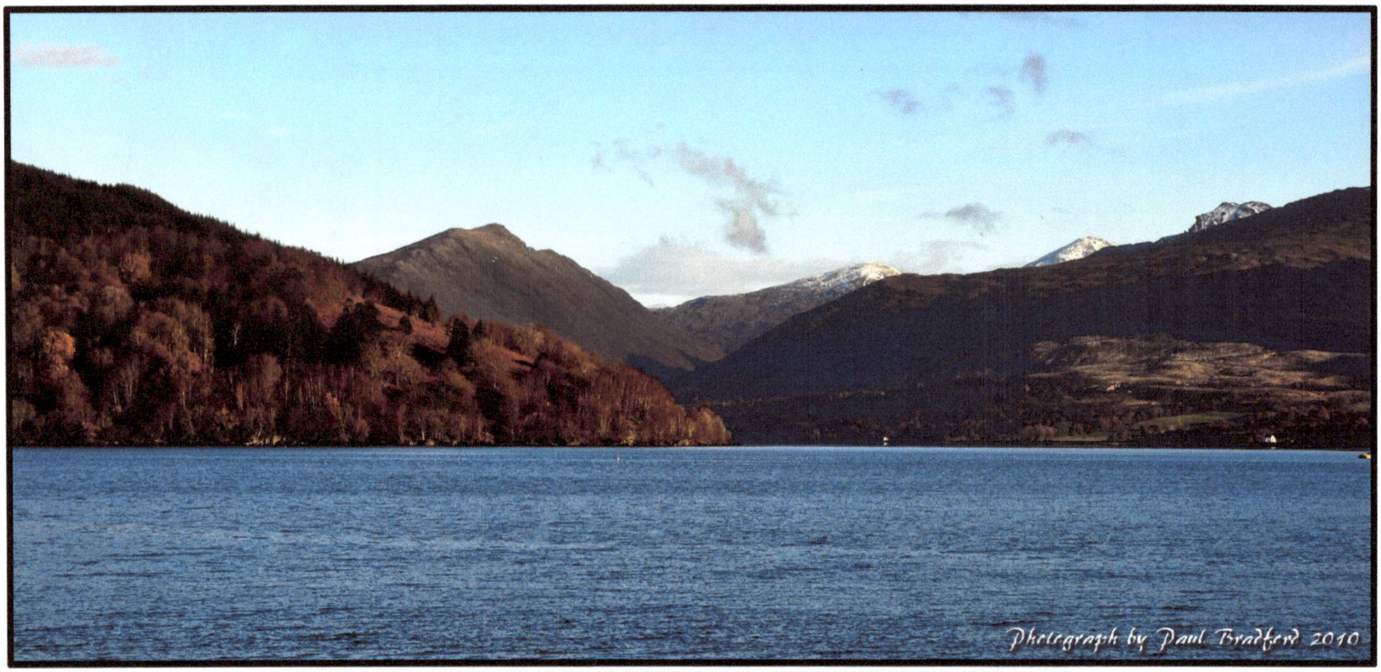

Photograph by Paul Bradford 2010

Loch Fyne

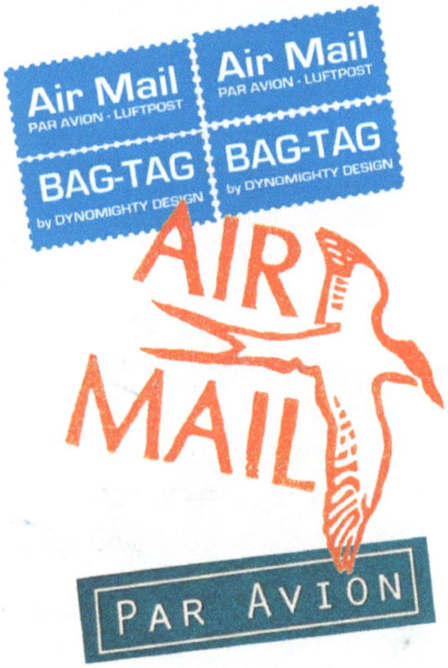

Air Mail
PAR AVION - LUFTPOST

Air Mail
PAR AVION - LUFTPOST

BAG-TAG
by DYNOMIGHTY DESIGN

BAG-TAG
by DYNOMIGHTY DESIGN

AIR MAIL

PAR AVION

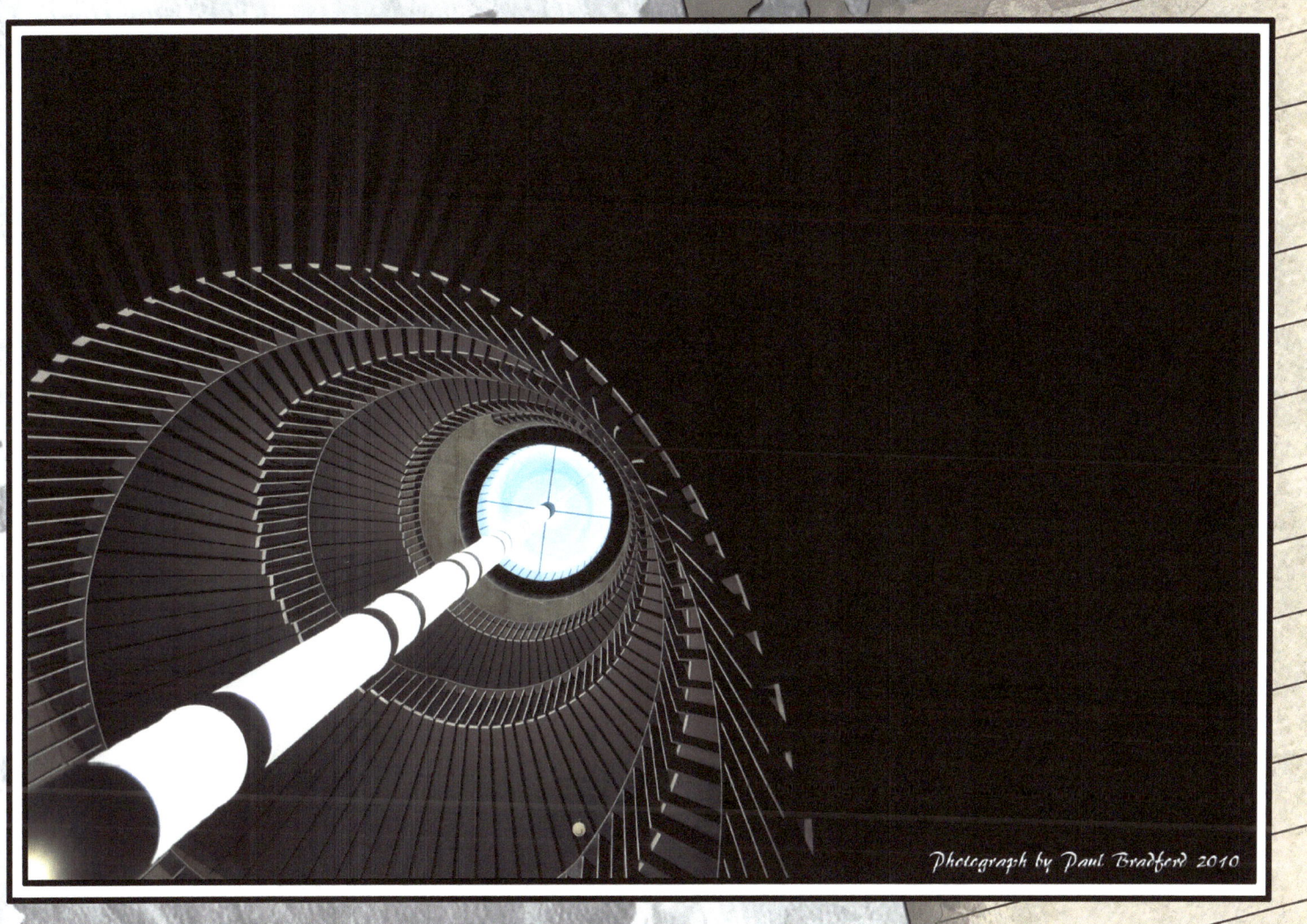

Photograph by Paul Bradford 2010

This picture is actually of a stair well at Usher Hall,
Edinburgh Scotland. What makes this particularly unique
is that the theatre itself is restored to reflect its
original look and style, but then there's this very futuristic
modern looking stairwell that looks like it belongs in the
engine room of the starship enterprise rather than a theatre

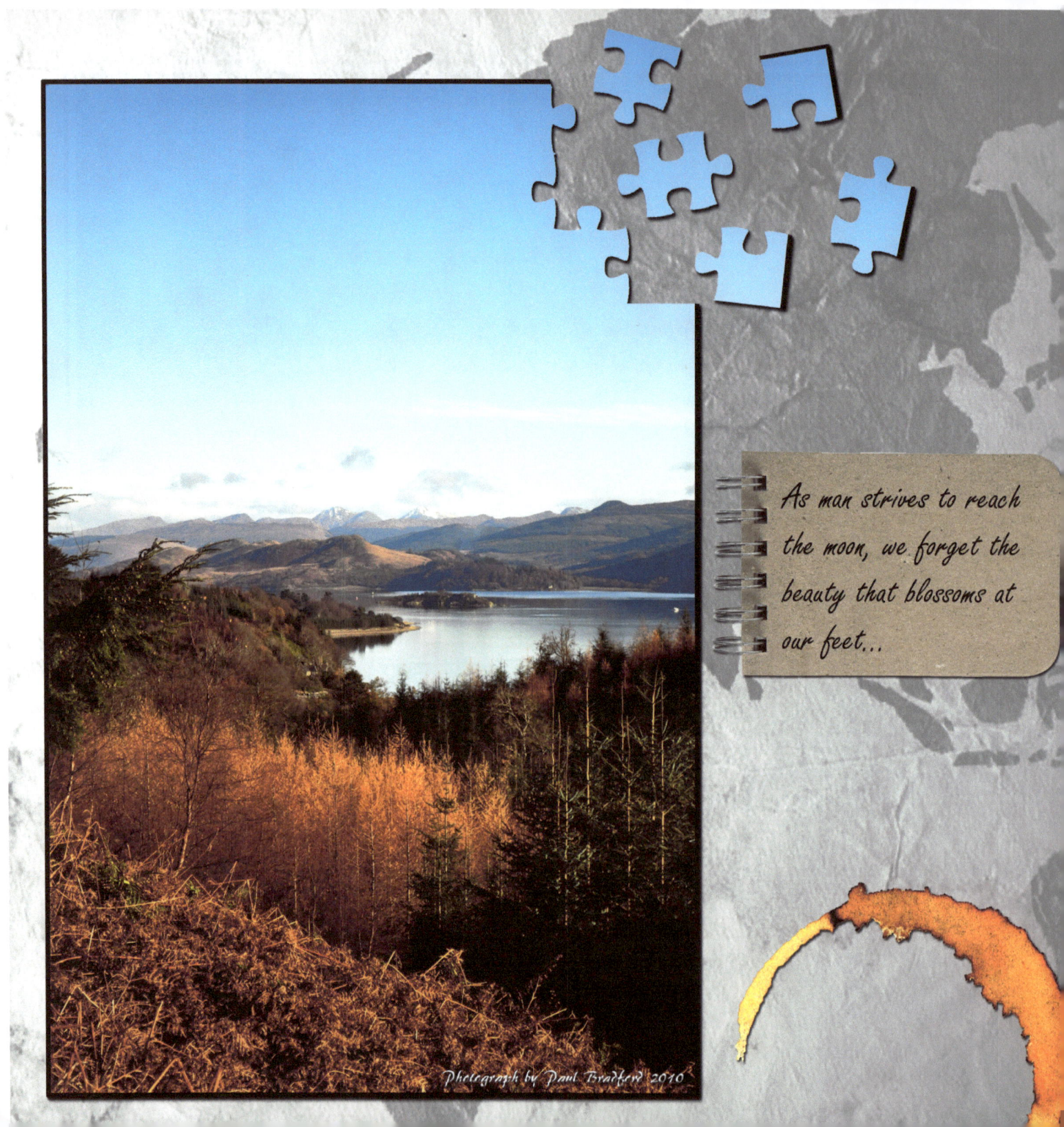

As man strives to reach the moon, we forget the beauty that blossoms at our feet...

Photograph by Paul Bradford 2010

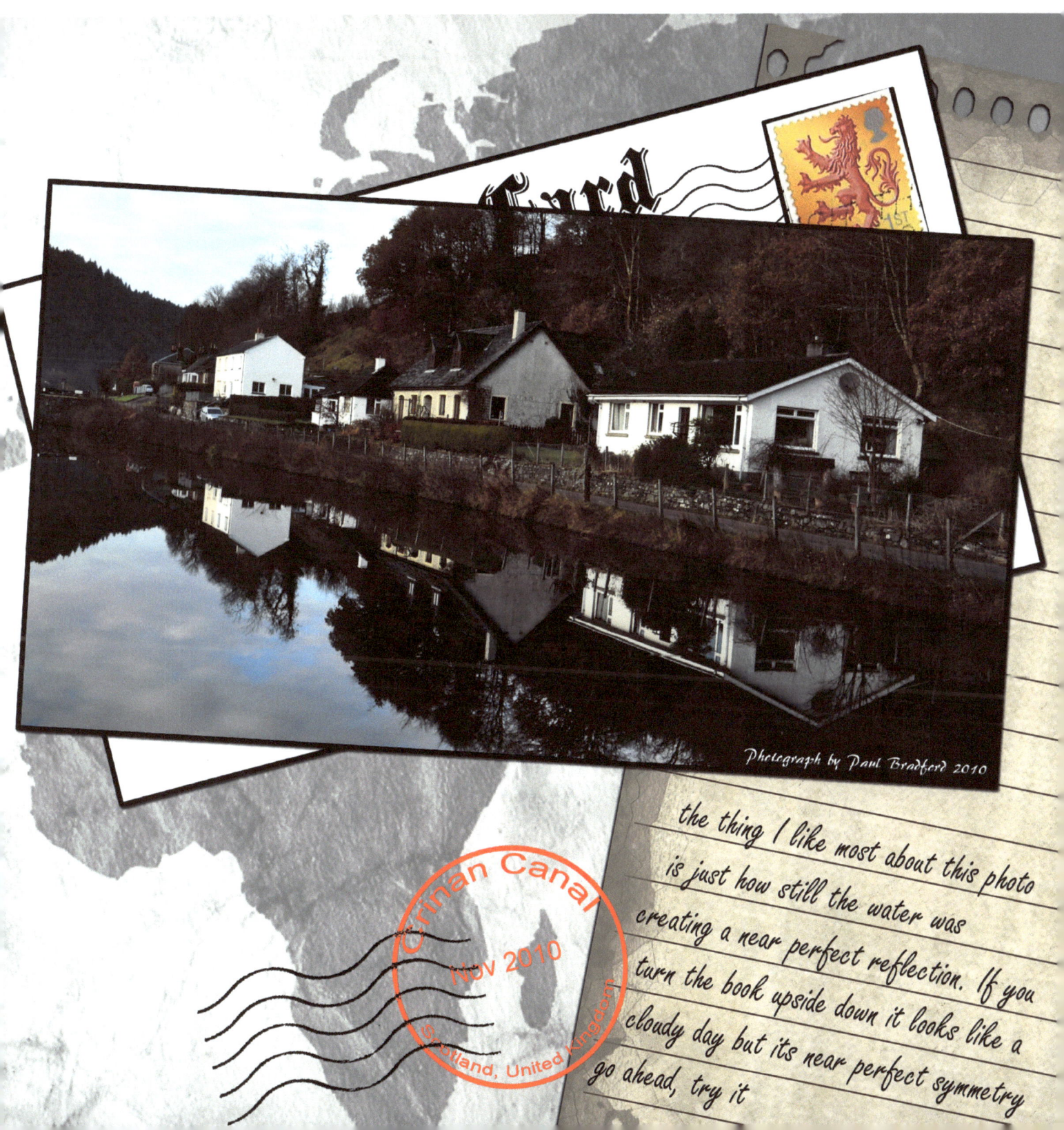

Photograph by Paul Bradford 2010

Crinan Canal
Nov 2010
Scotland, United Kingdom

the thing I like most about this photo
is just how still the water was
creating a near perfect reflection. If you
turn the book upside down it looks like a
cloudy day but its near perfect symmetry
go ahead, try it

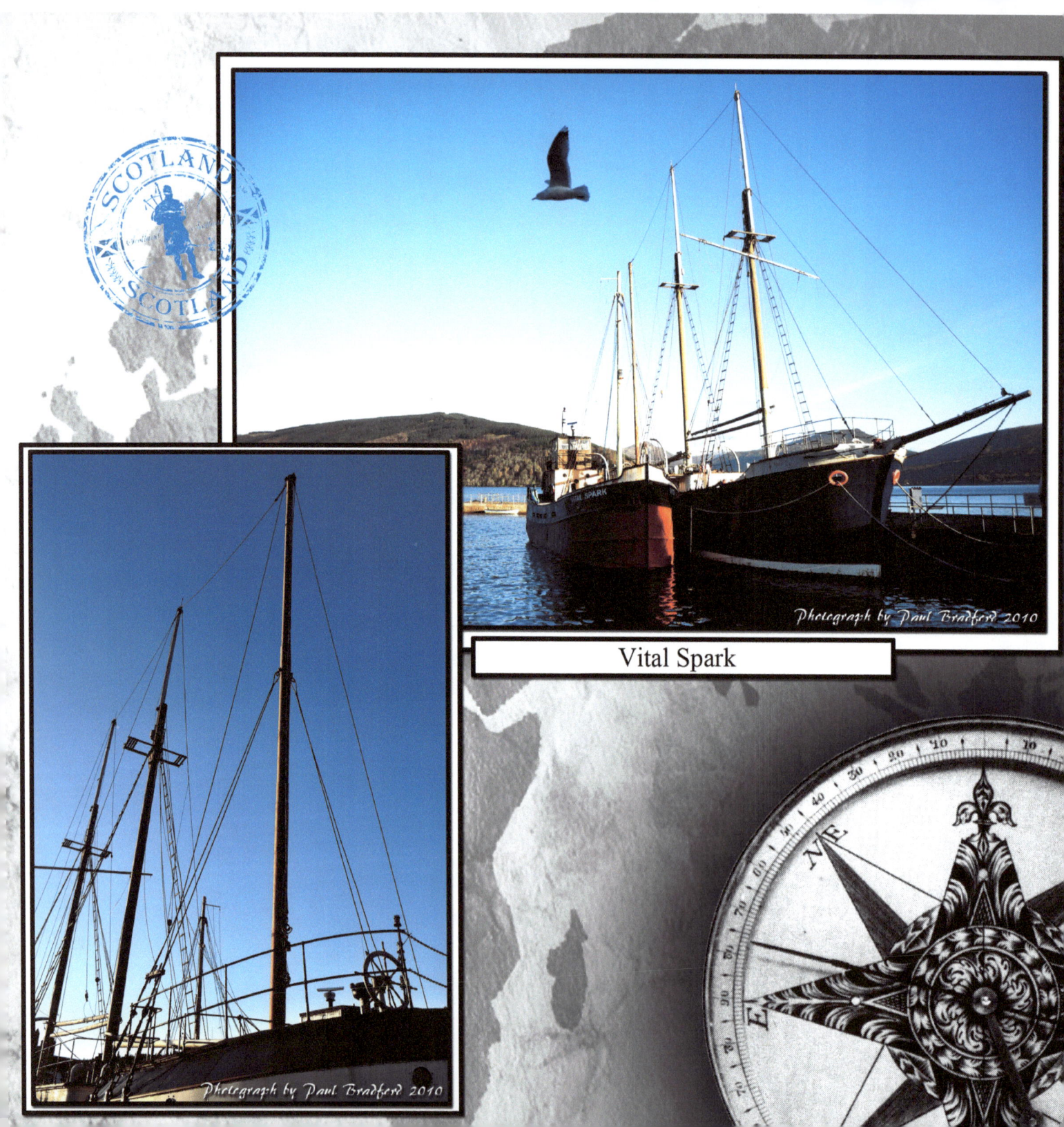

Vital Spark

Photograph by Paul Bradford 2010

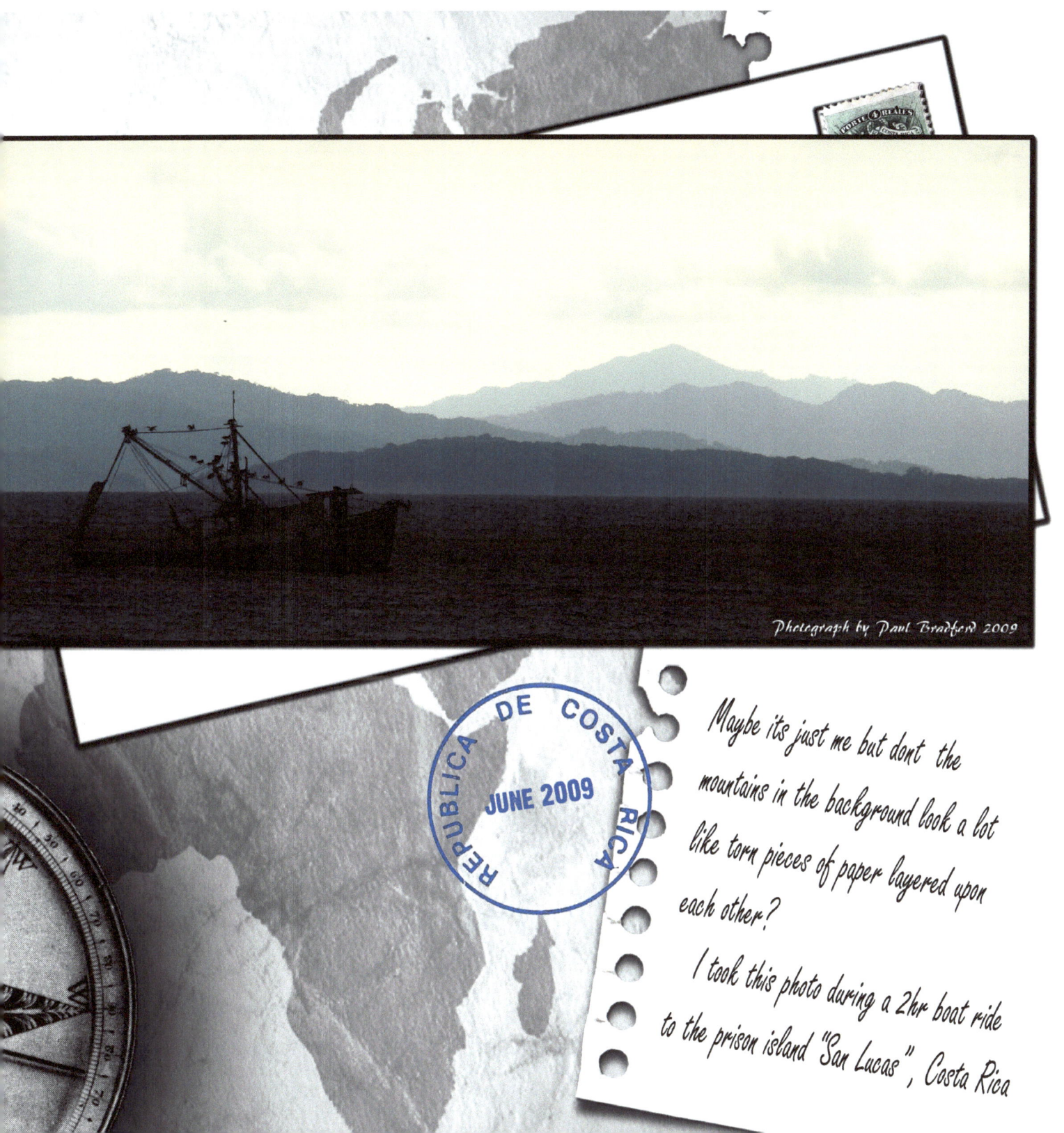

Photograph by Paul Bradford 2009

REPUBLICA DE COSTA RICA

JUNE 2009

Maybe its just me but dont the mountains in the background look a lot like torn pieces of paper layered upon each other?

I took this photo during a 2hr boat ride to the prison island "San Lucas", Costa Rica

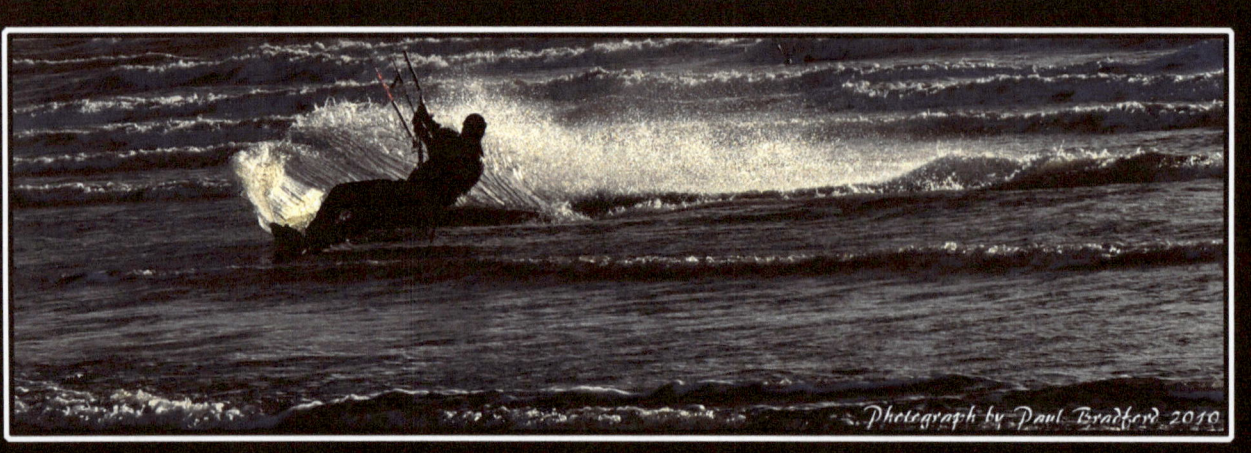

Photograph by Paul Bradford 2010

Extreme Sports

because not everyone can throw a ball or run fast

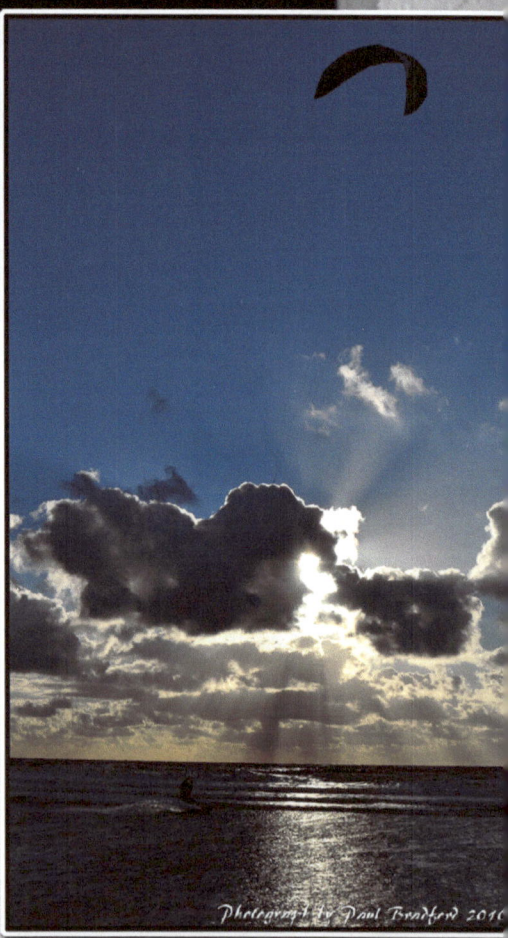

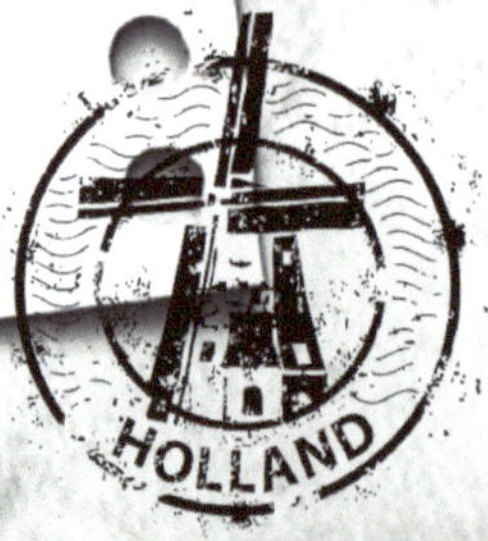

Photograph by Paul Bradford 2010

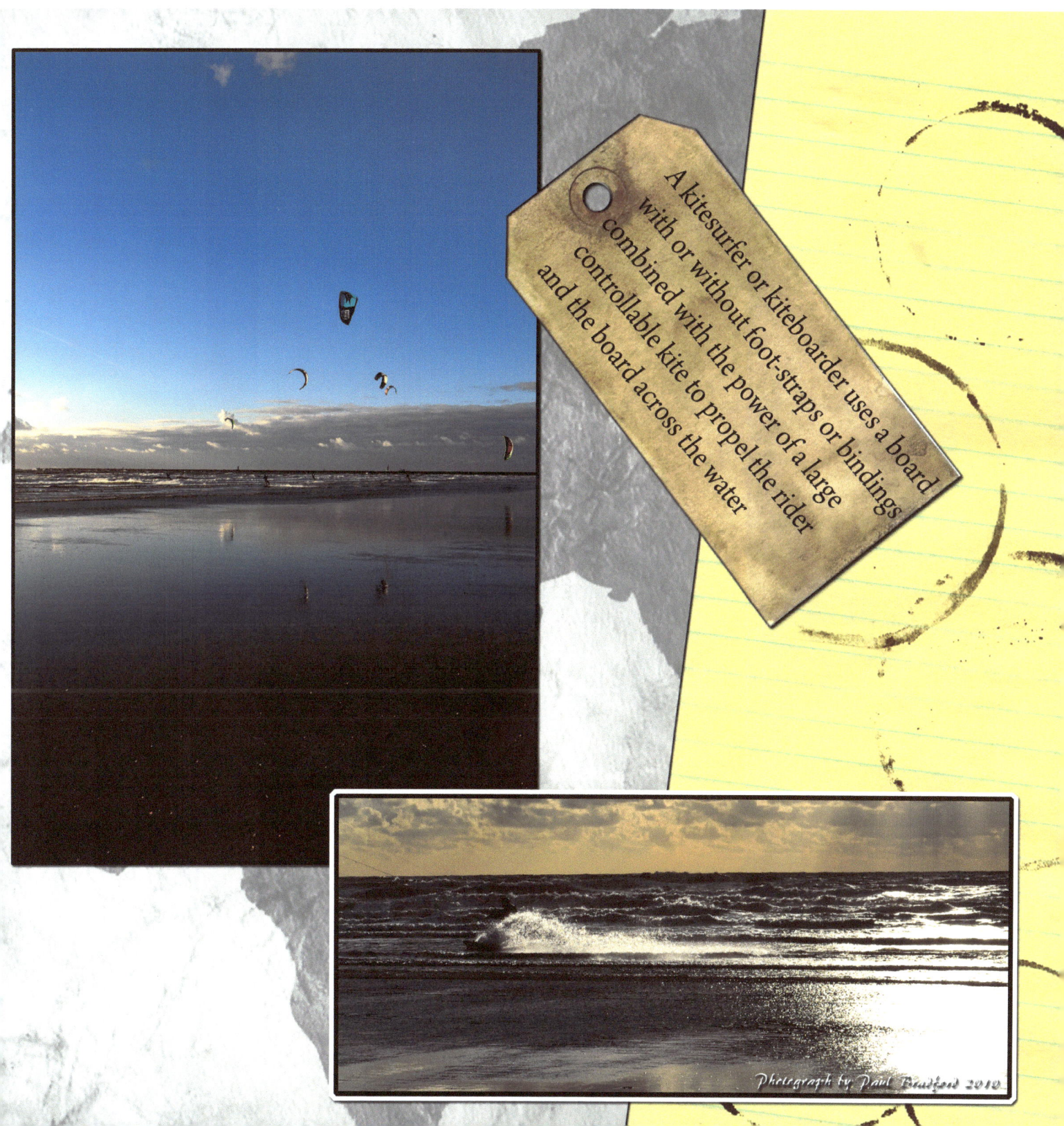

A kitesurfer or kiteboarder uses a board with or without foot-straps or bindings, combined with the power of a large controllable kite to propel the rider and the board across the water

Photograph by Paul Bradford 2010

Las garitas de Puerto Rico/sentry box is one of the national monuments in the island. Constructed by the Spaniards 500 hundred years ago.

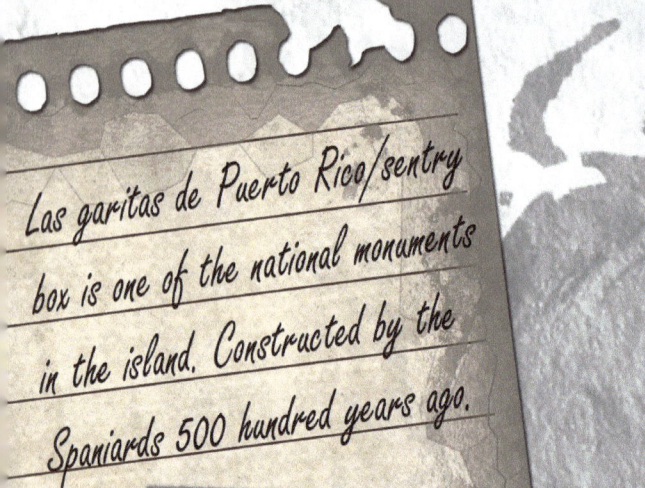

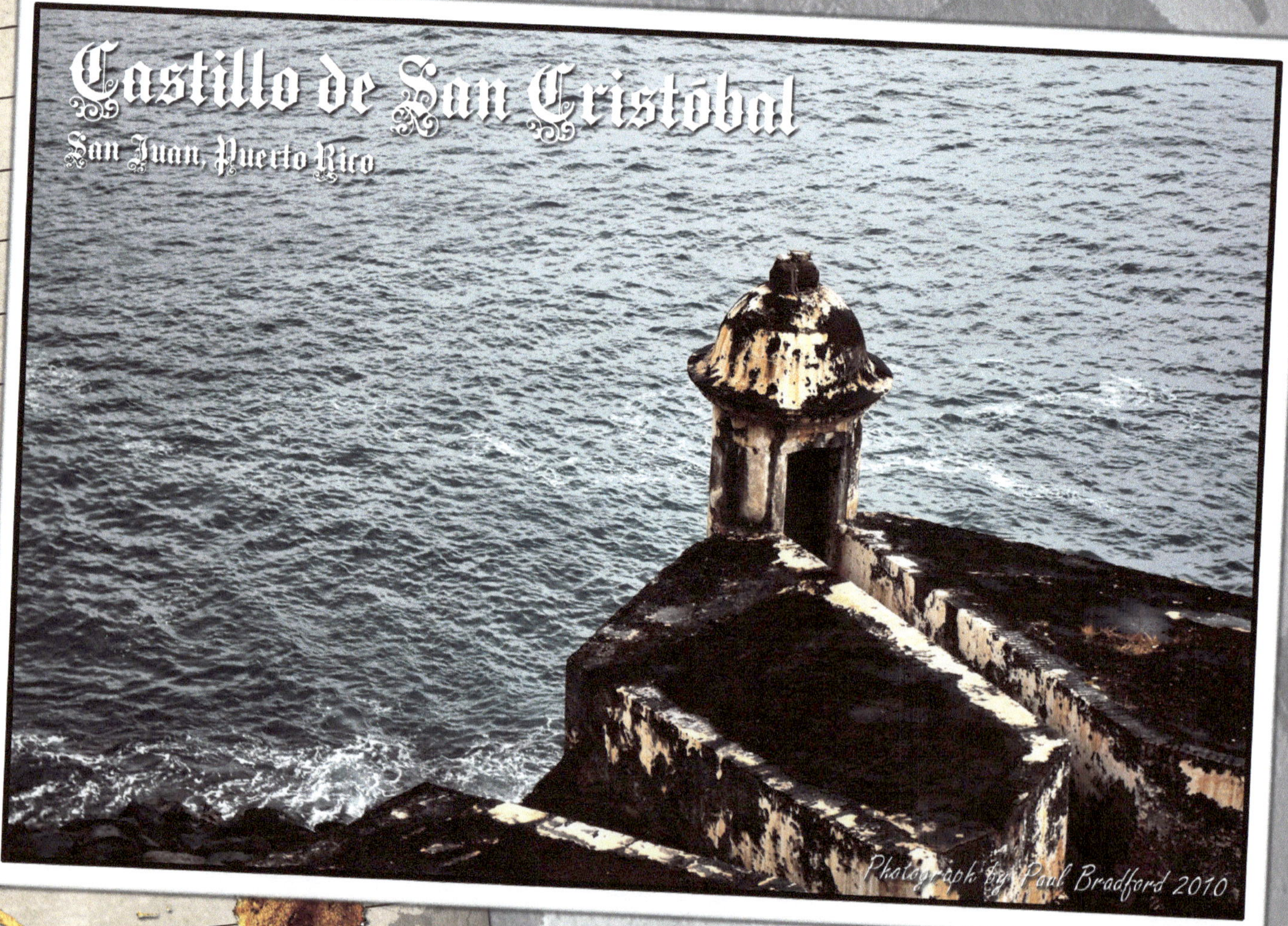

Castillo de San Cristóbal
San Juan, Puerto Rico

Photograph by Paul Bradford 2010

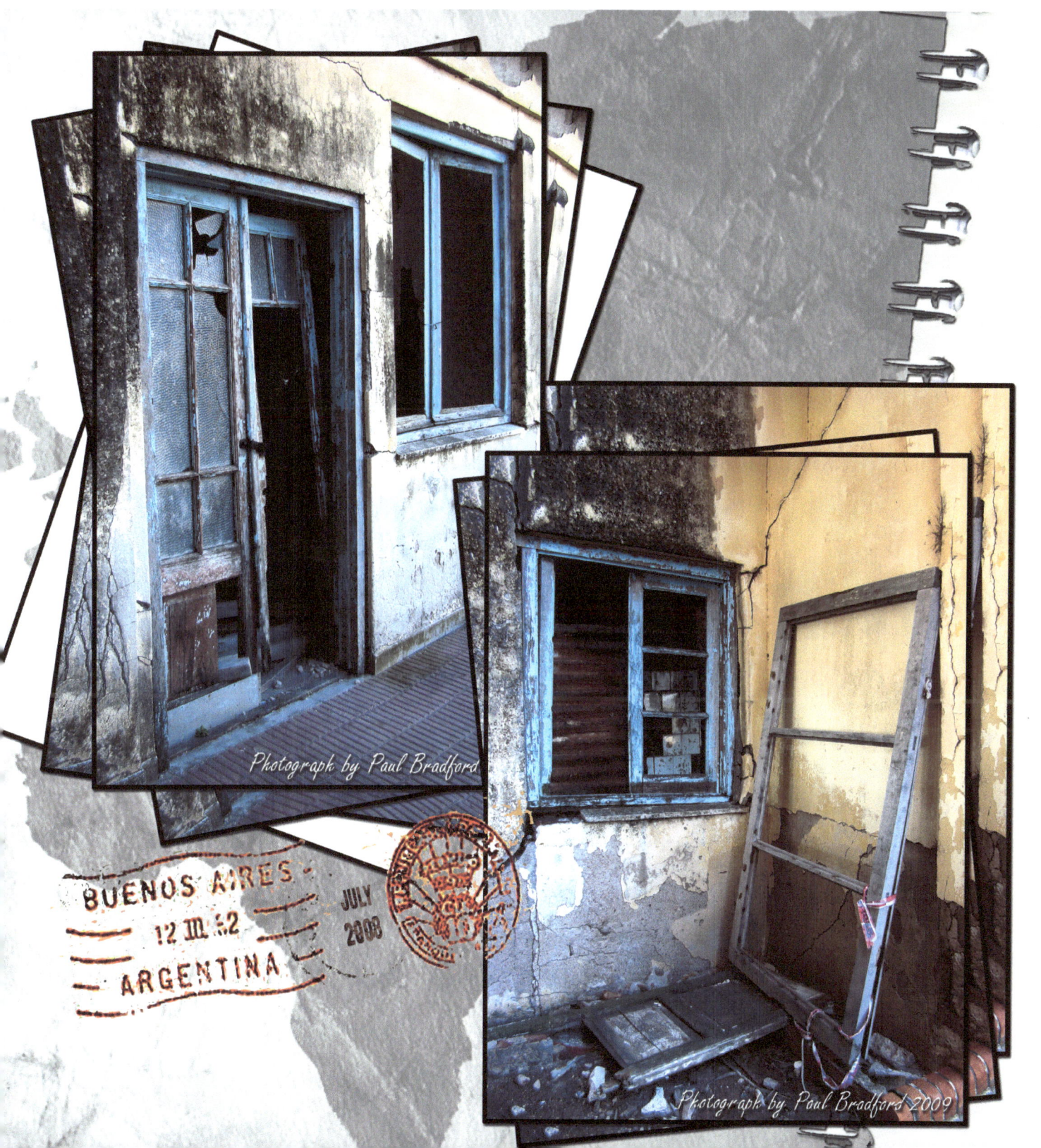

Photograph by Paul Bradford

BUENOS AIRES
12 III 52
ARGENTINA

JULY
2008

Photograph by Paul Bradford 2009

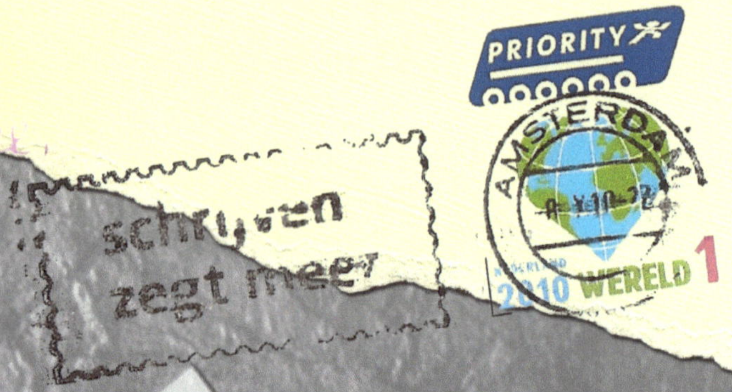

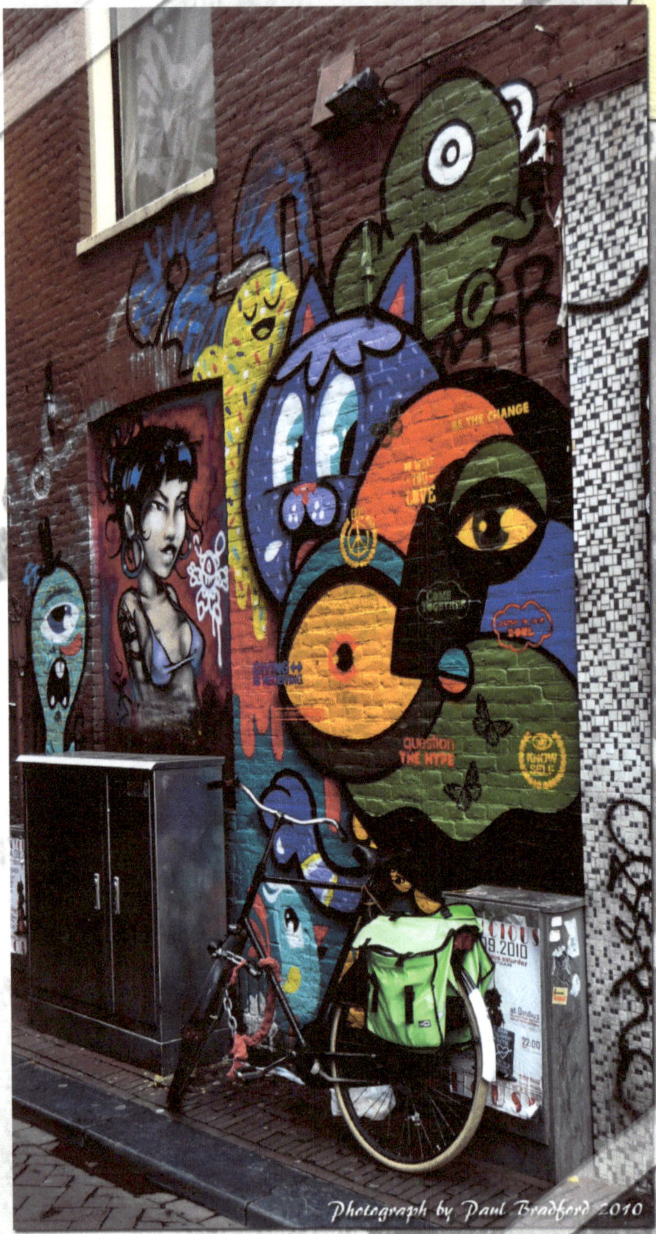

PRIORITY

AMSTERDAM
2010 WERELD 1

schrijven
zegt meer

Photograph by Paul Bradford 2010

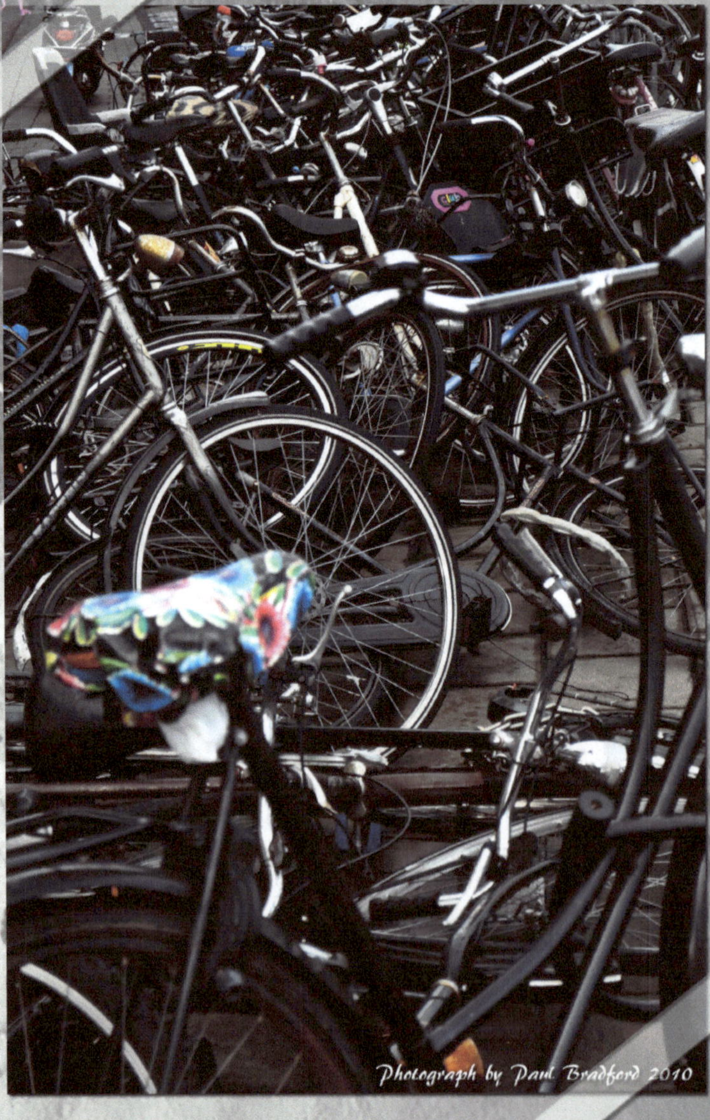

Photograph by Paul Bradford 2010

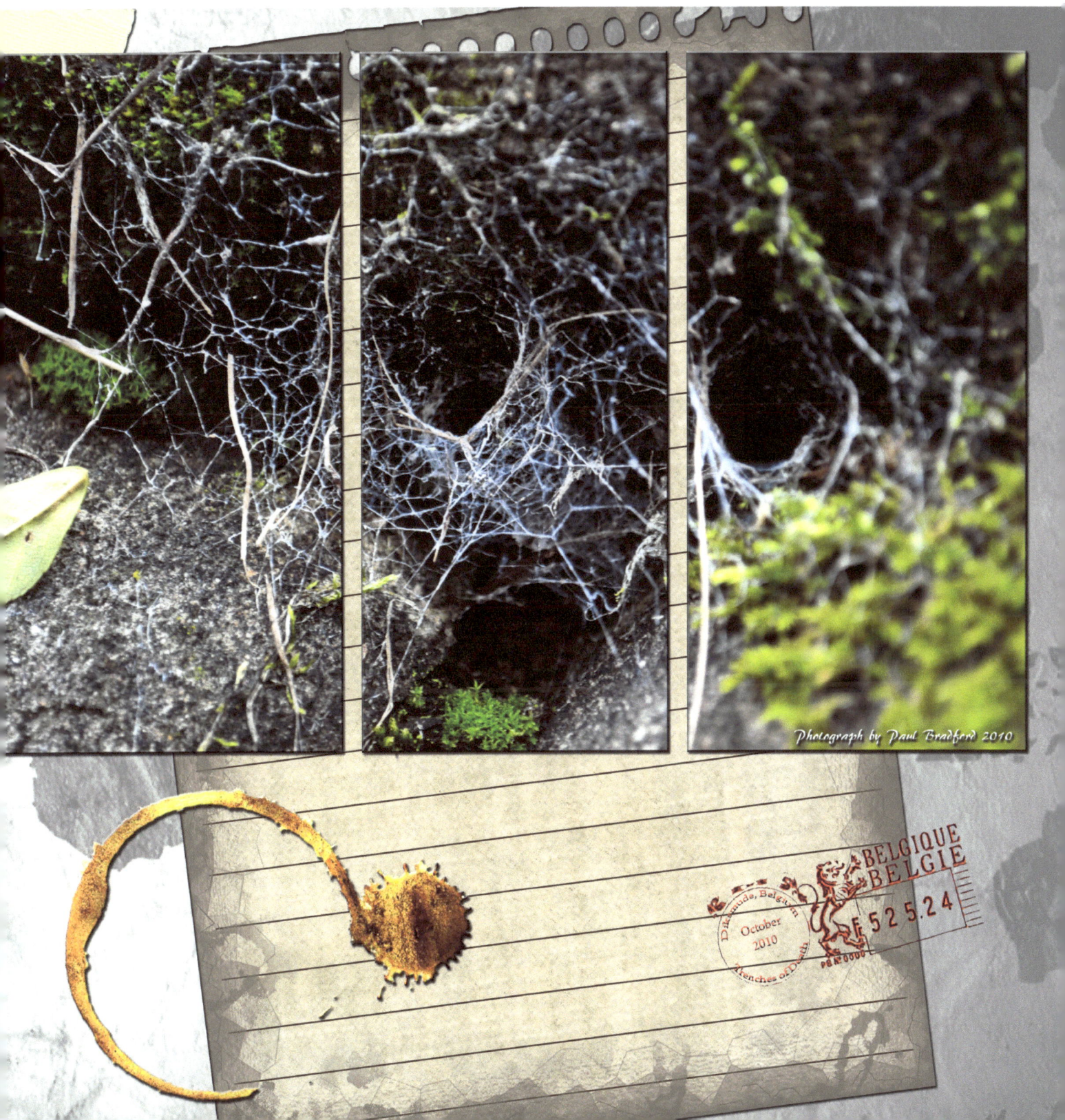

Photograph by Paul Bradford 2010

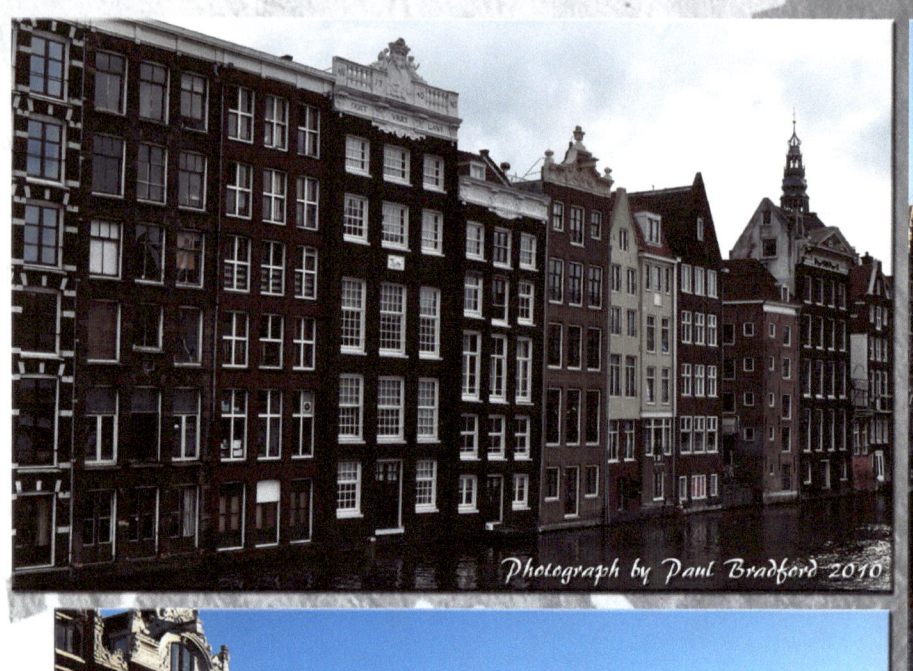

Photograph by Paul Bradford 2010

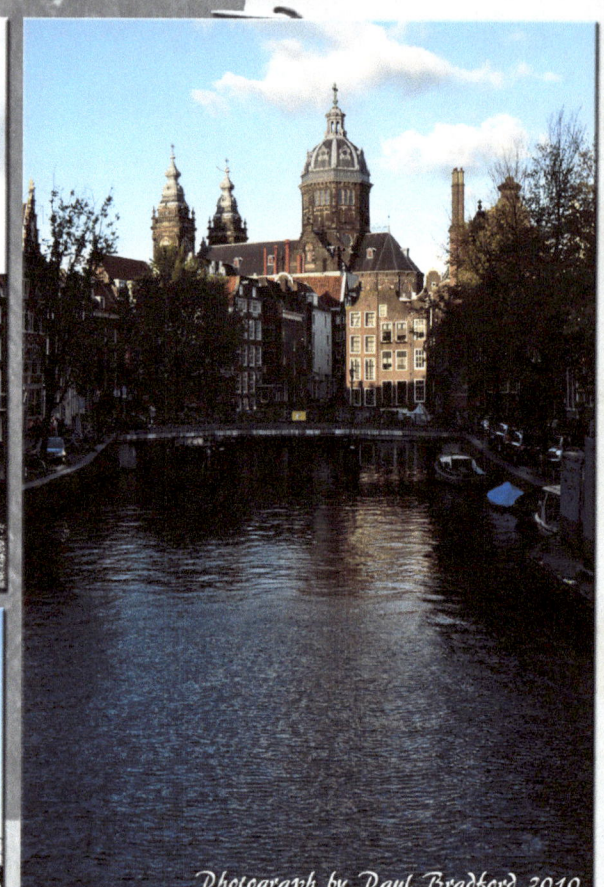

Photograph by Paul Bradford 2010

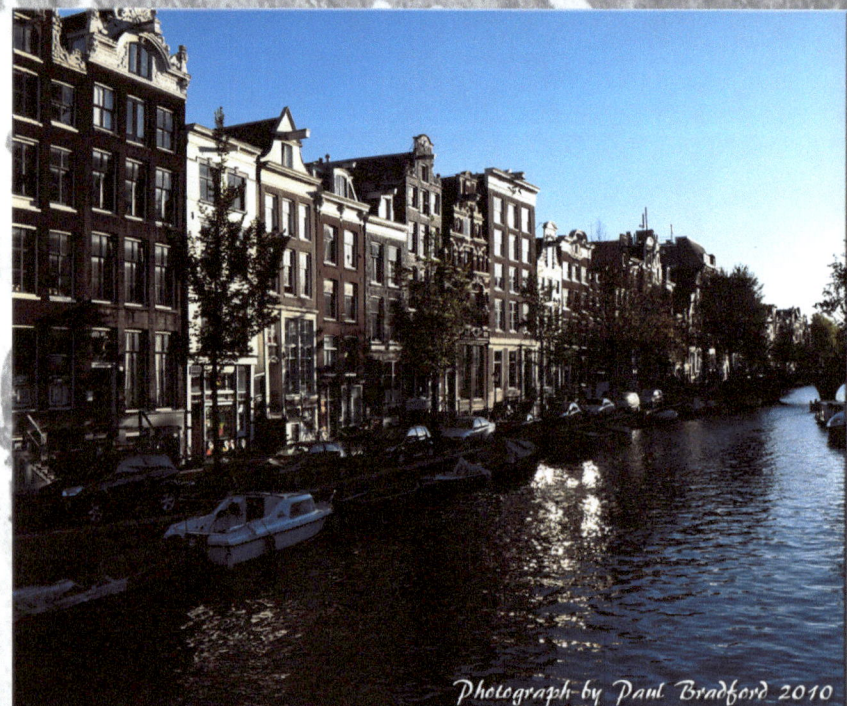

Photograph by Paul Bradford 2010

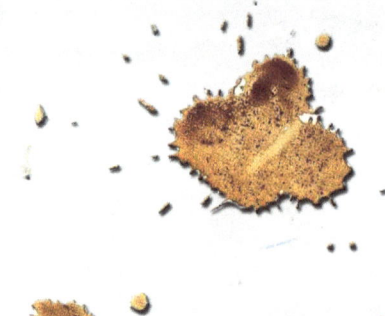

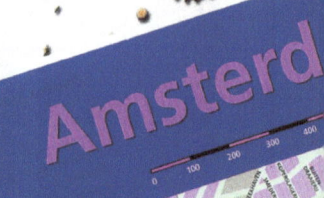

Amsterd

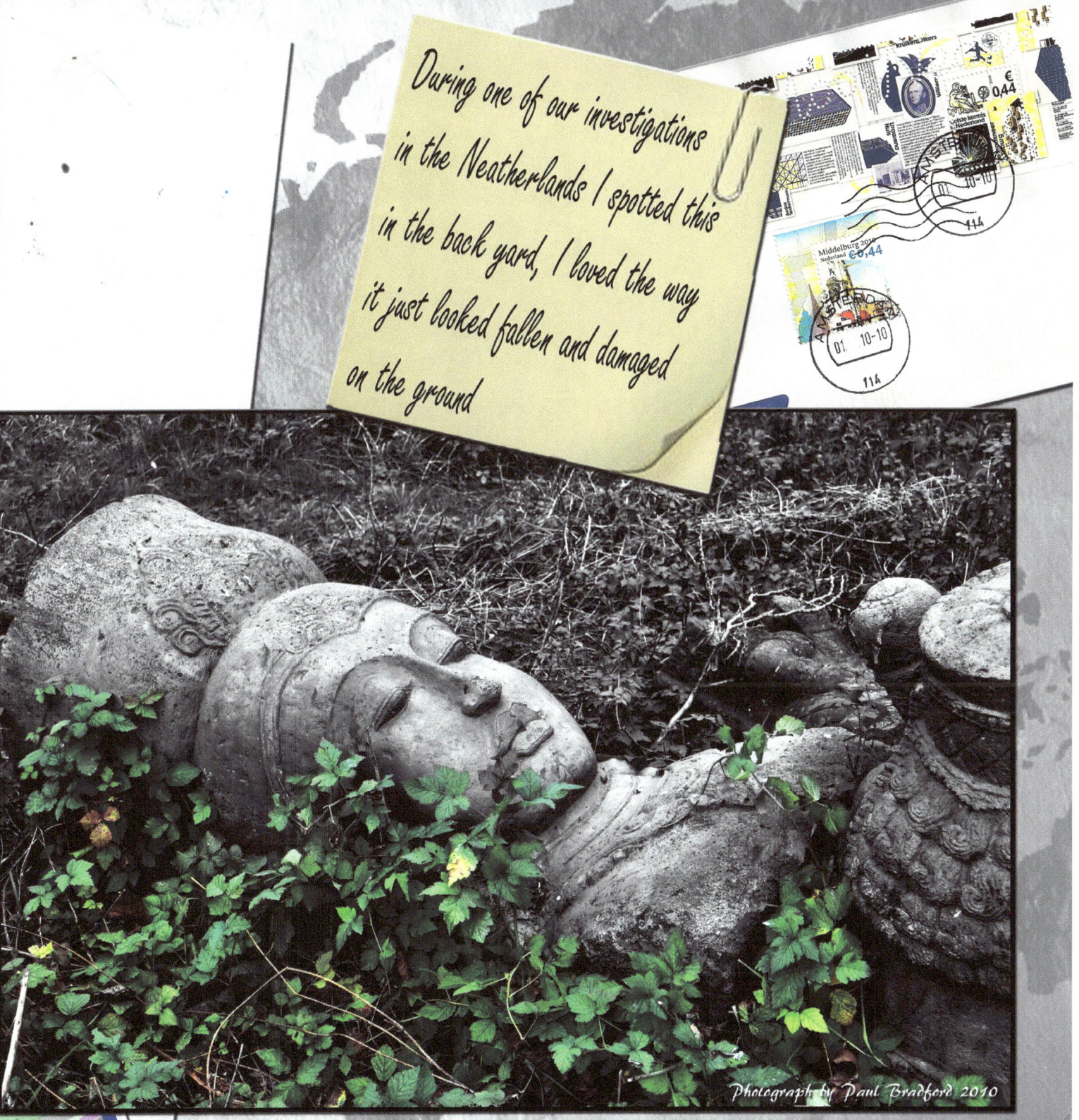

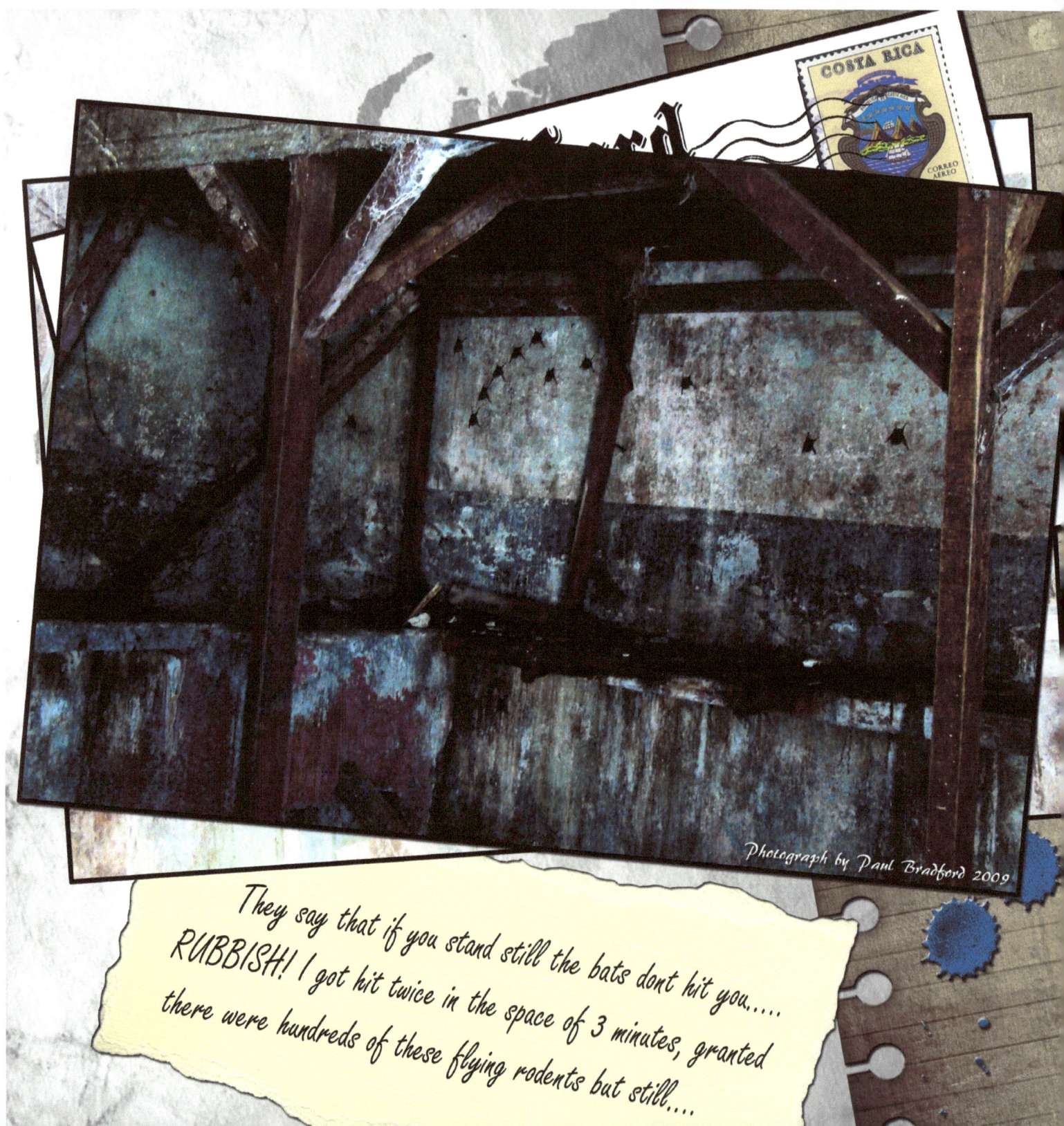

COSTA RICA

CORREO AEREO

Photograph by Paul Bradford 2009

They say that if you stand still the bats dont hit you.....
RUBBISH! I got hit twice in the space of 3 minutes, granted
there were hundreds of these flying rodents but still....

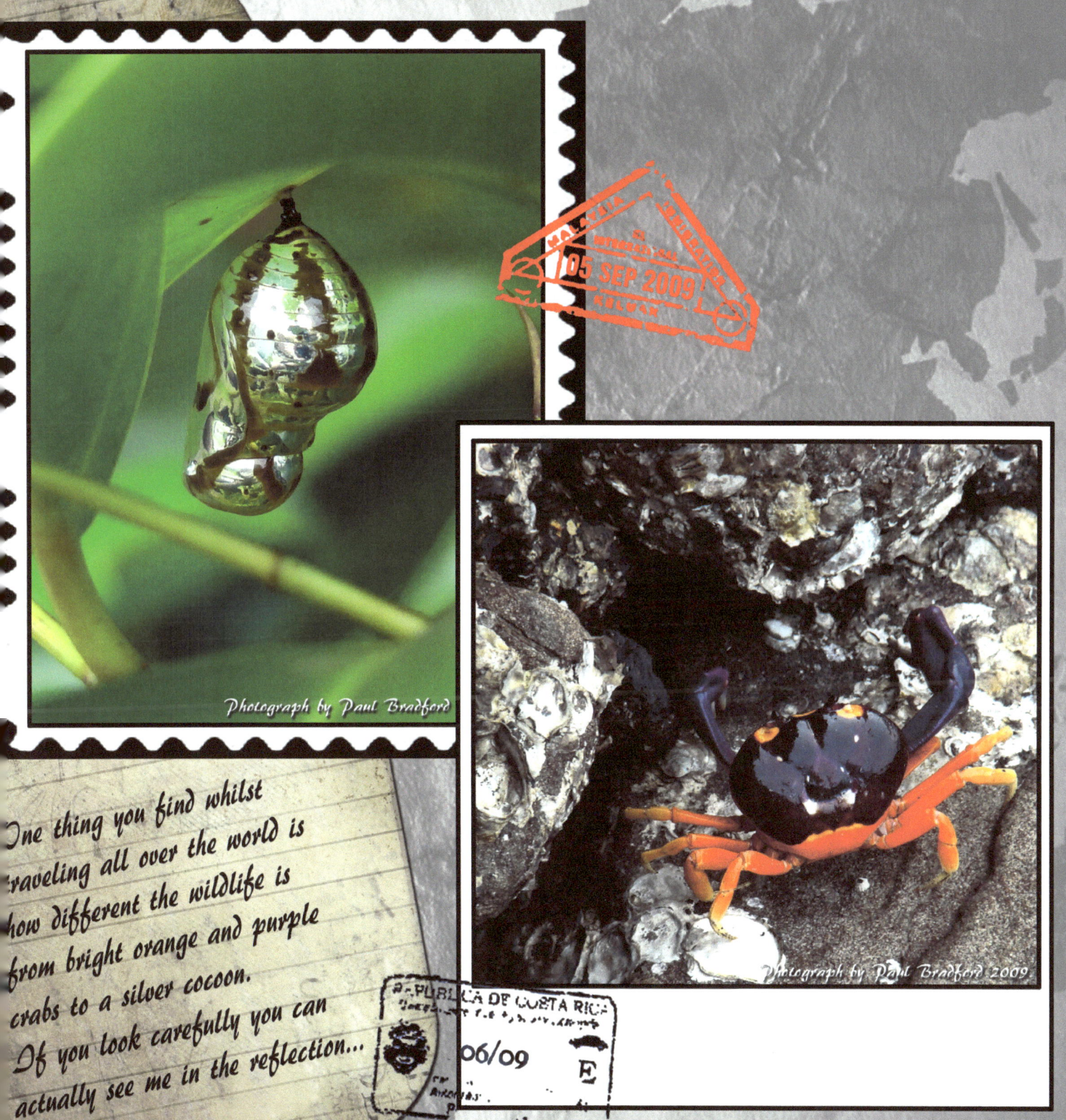

Photograph by Paul Bradford

05 SEP 2009

Photograph by Paul Bradford 2009

One thing you find whilst traveling all over the world is how different the wildlife is from bright orange and purple crabs to a silver cocoon.
If you look carefully you can actually see me in the reflection...

REPUBLICA DE COSTA RICA

06/09   E

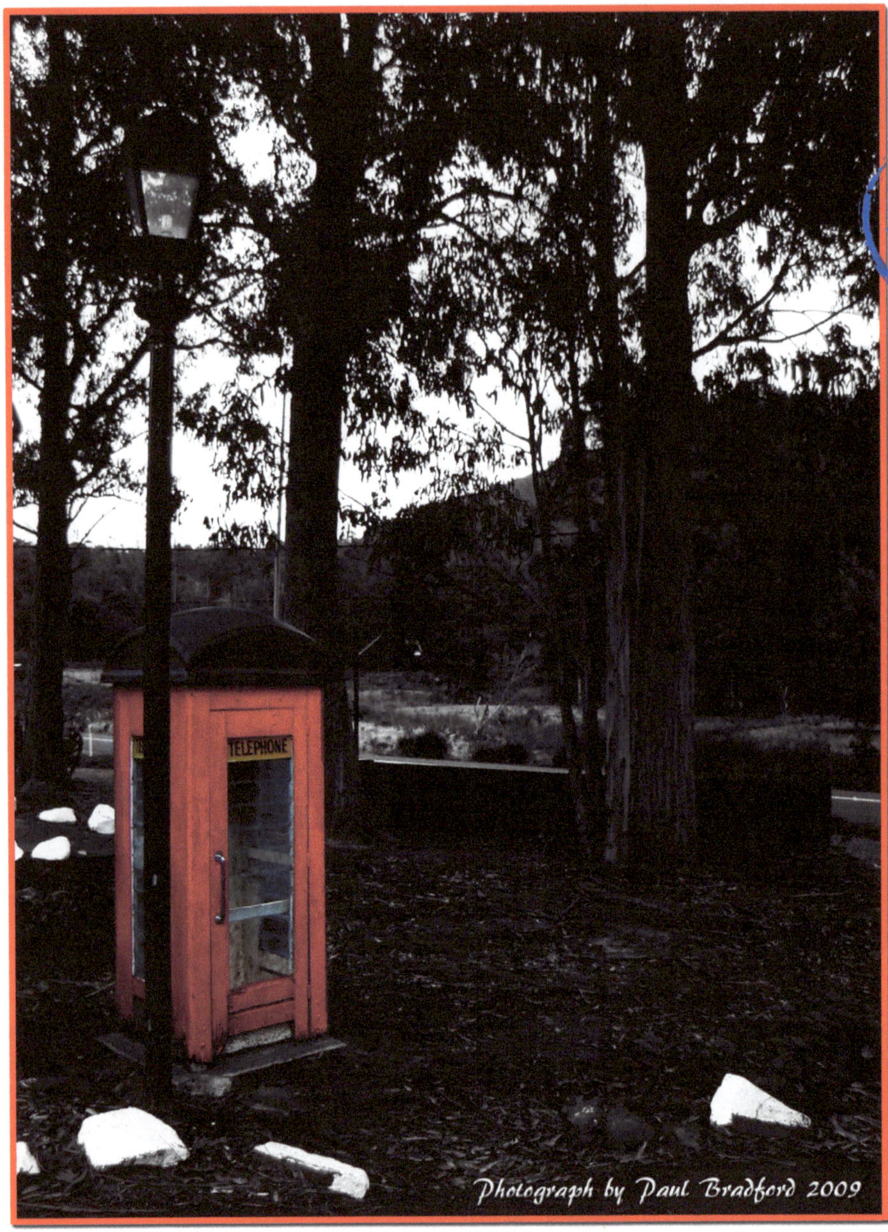

Photograph by Paul Bradford 2009

Tasmania

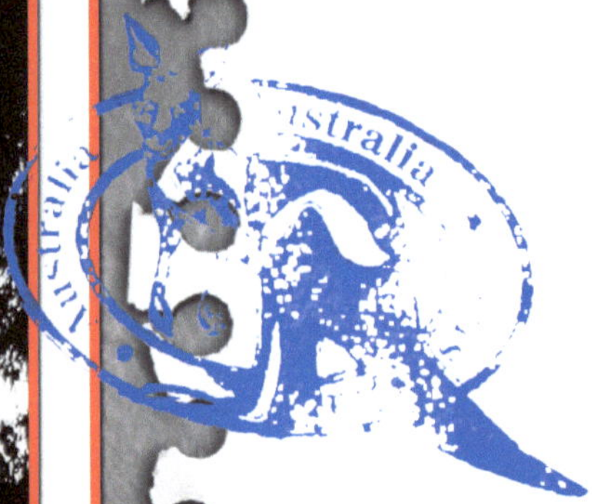

The Tasmanian Devil
- ugly, smelly and
eats everything...

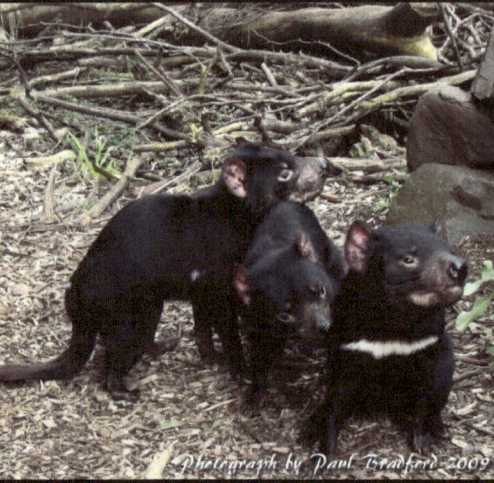

Photograph by Paul Bradford 2009

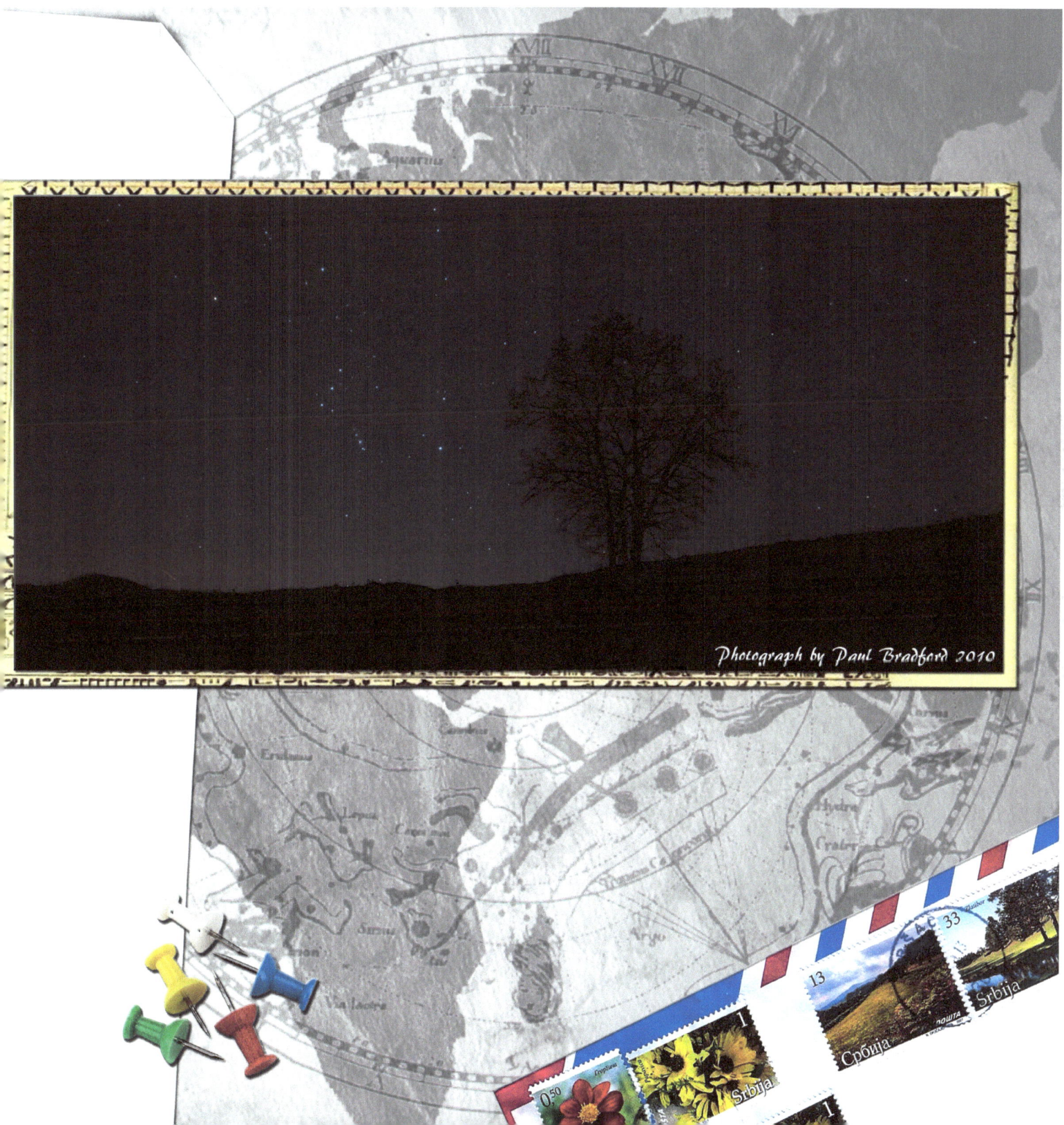

Photograph by Paul Bradford 2010

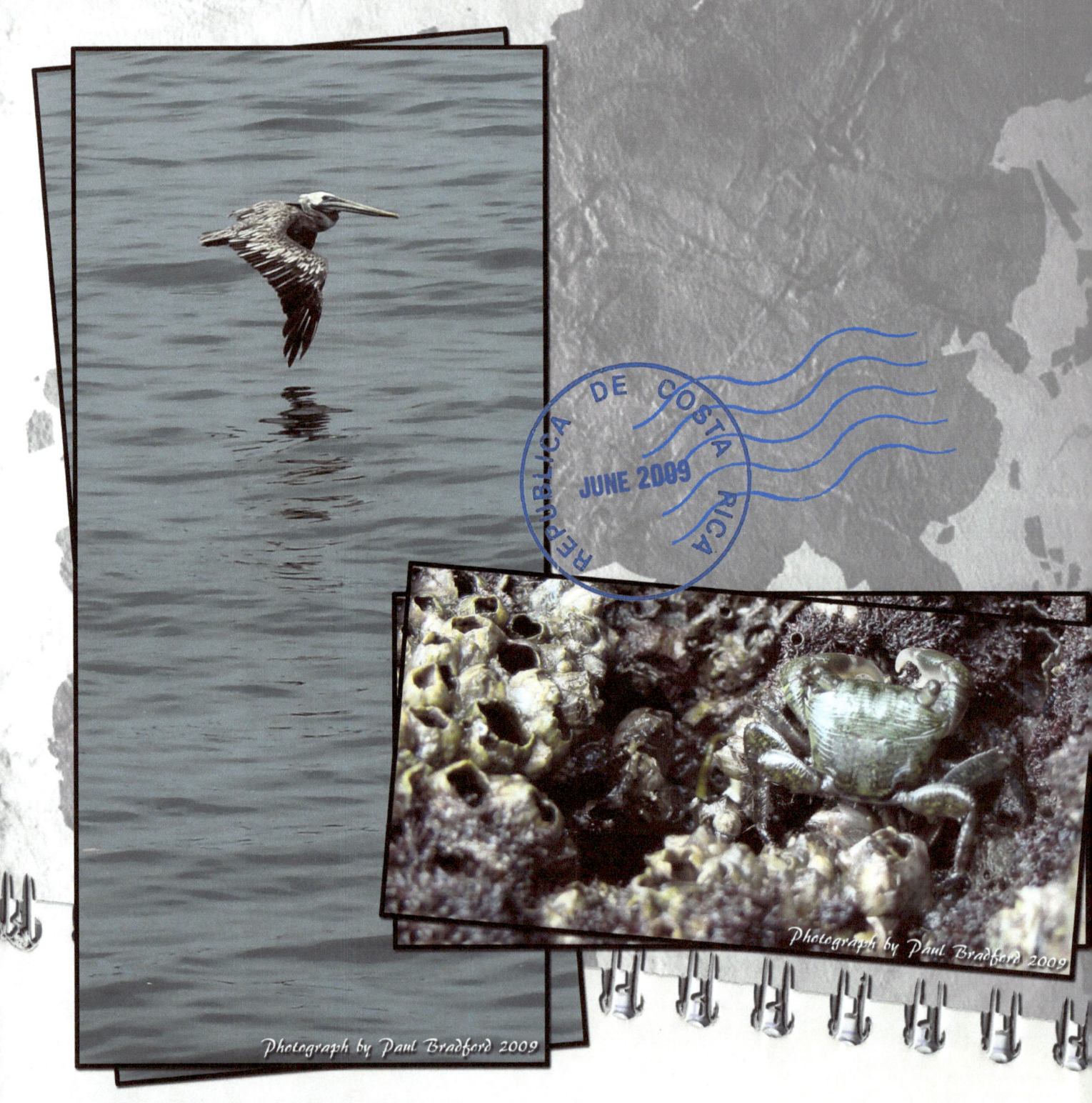

REPUBLICA DE COSTA RICA

JUNE 2009

Photograph by Paul Bradford 2009

Photograph by Paul Bradford 2009

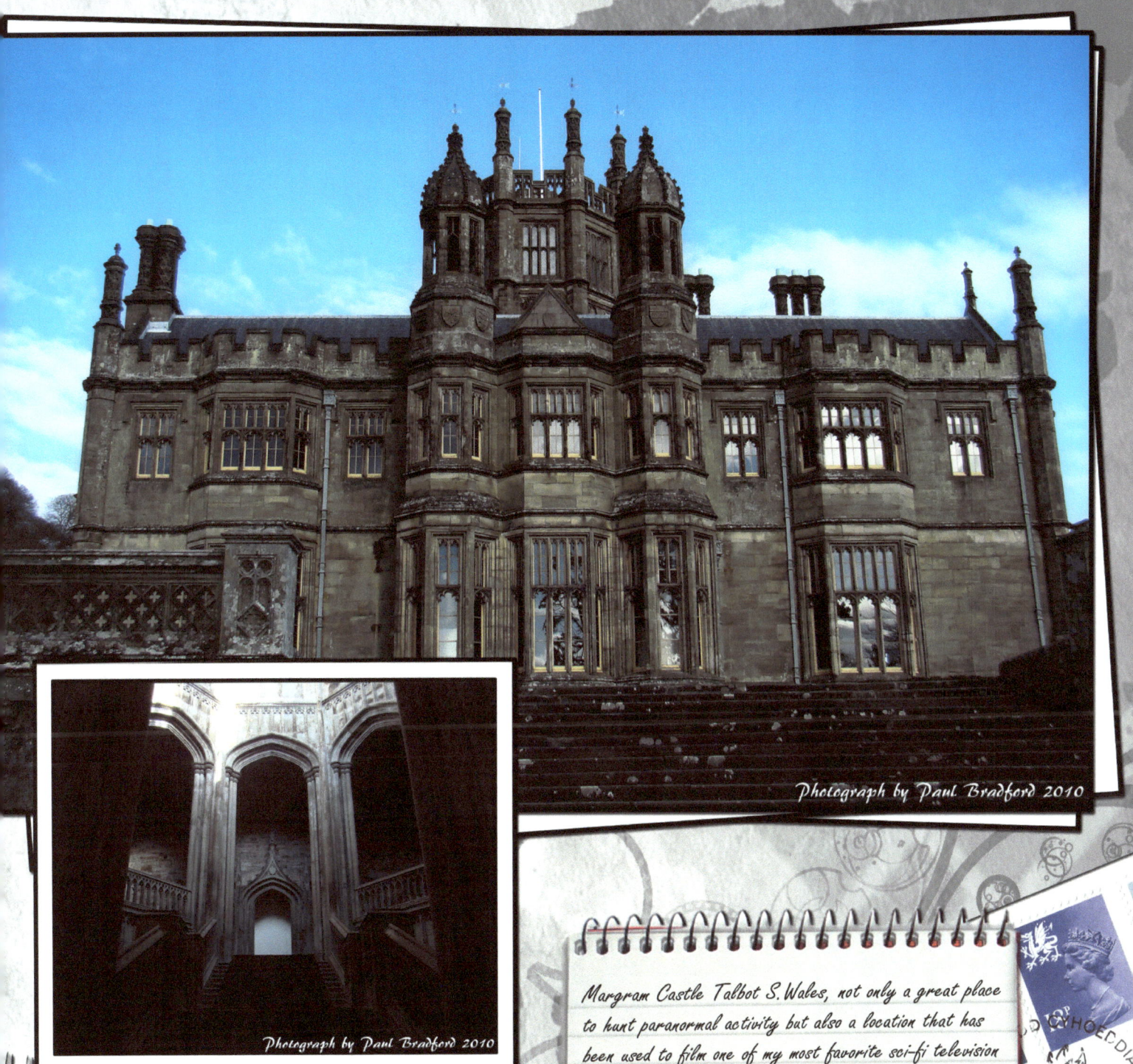

Photograph by Paul Bradford 2010

Photograph by Paul Bradford 2010

Margram Castle Talbot S. Wales, not only a great place to hunt paranormal activity but also a location that has been used to film one of my most favorite sci-fi television shows of all time (and space), Doctor Who.

It actually took ten years to build this "Castle" which is really more a Victorian era country house 1830-1840

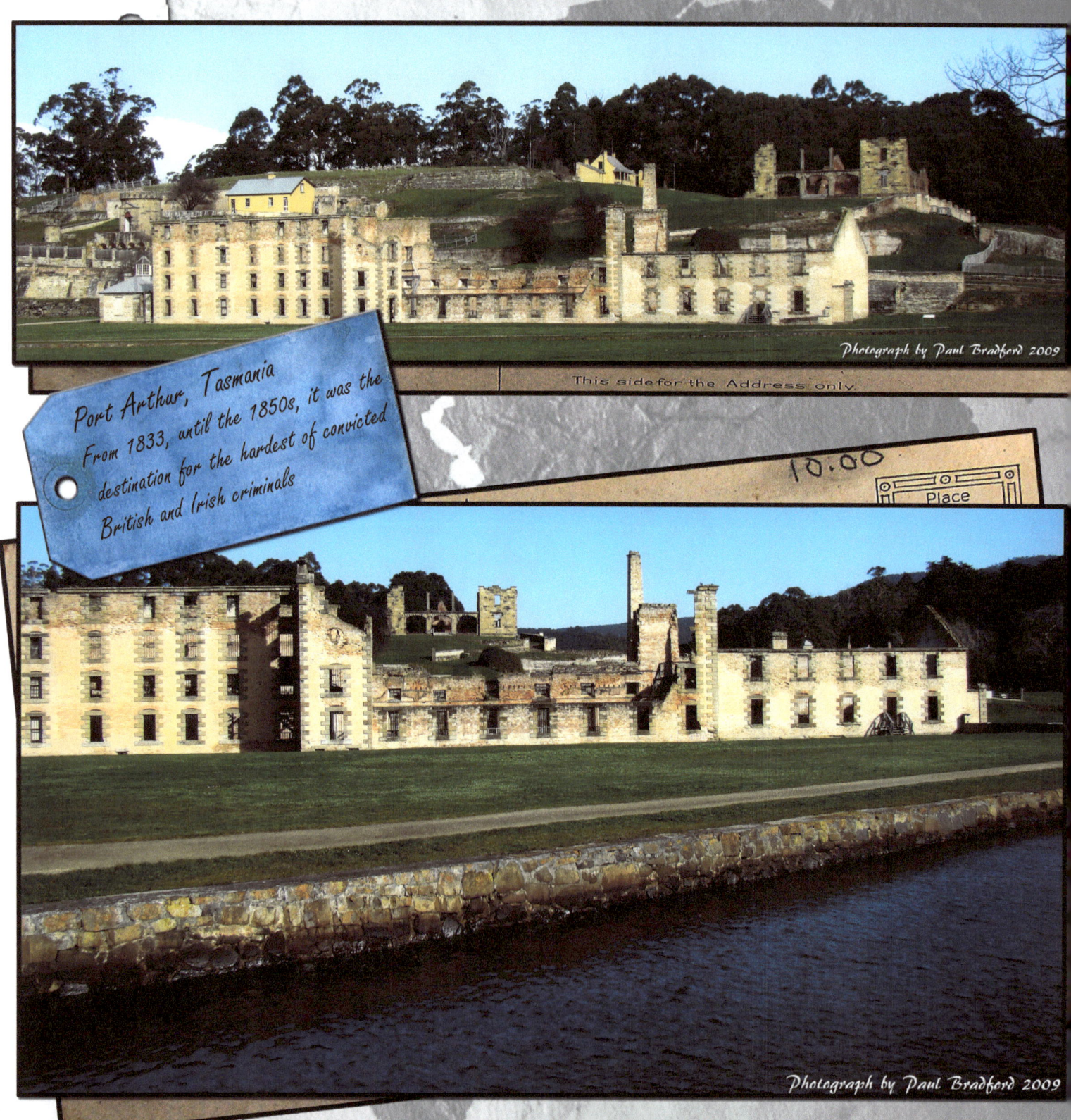

Port Arthur, Tasmania

From 1833, until the 1850s, it was the destination for the hardest of convicted British and Irish criminals

This side for the Address only.

Photograph by Paul Bradford 2009

10.00

Place

Photograph by Paul Bradford 2009

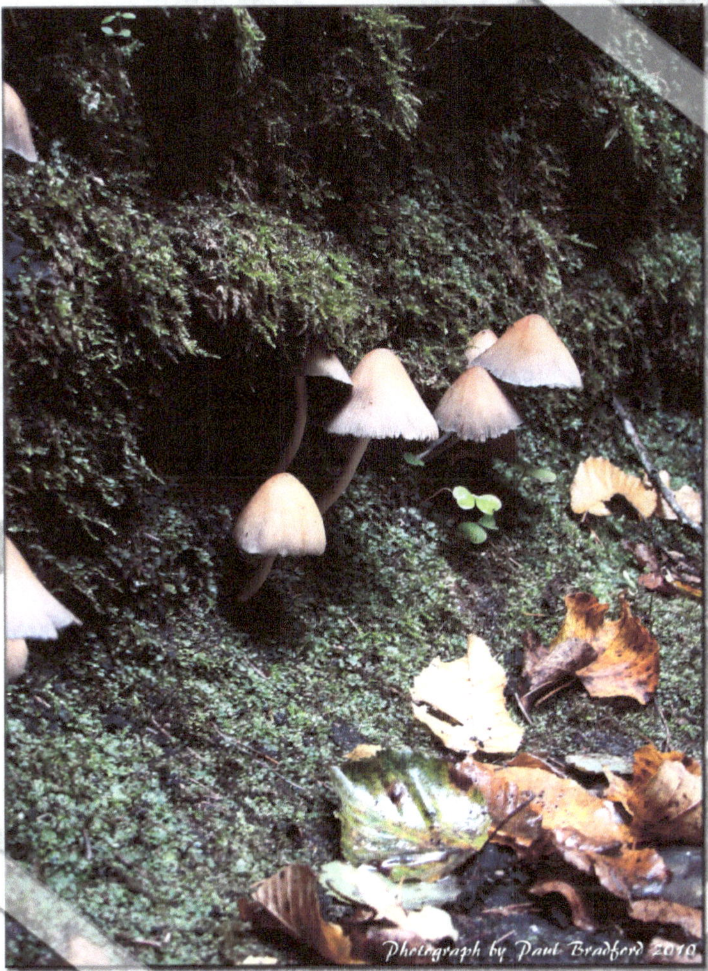

Photograph by Paul Bradford 2010

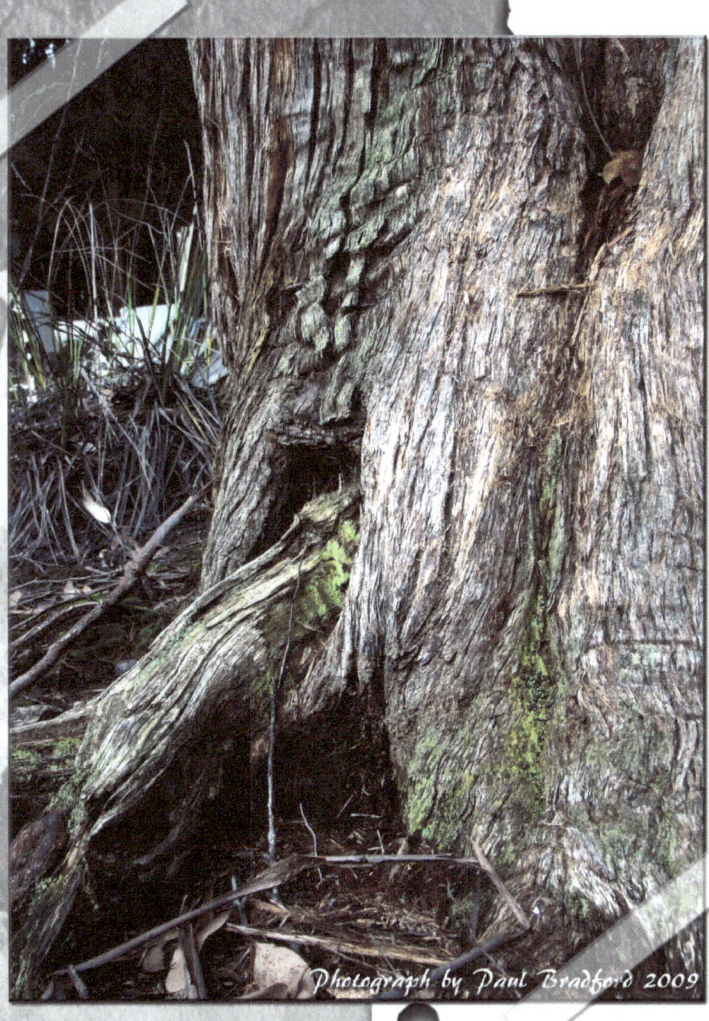

*Nature does not hurry,
yet everything is accomplished.*

- Lao Tzu

Photograph by Paul Bradford 2009

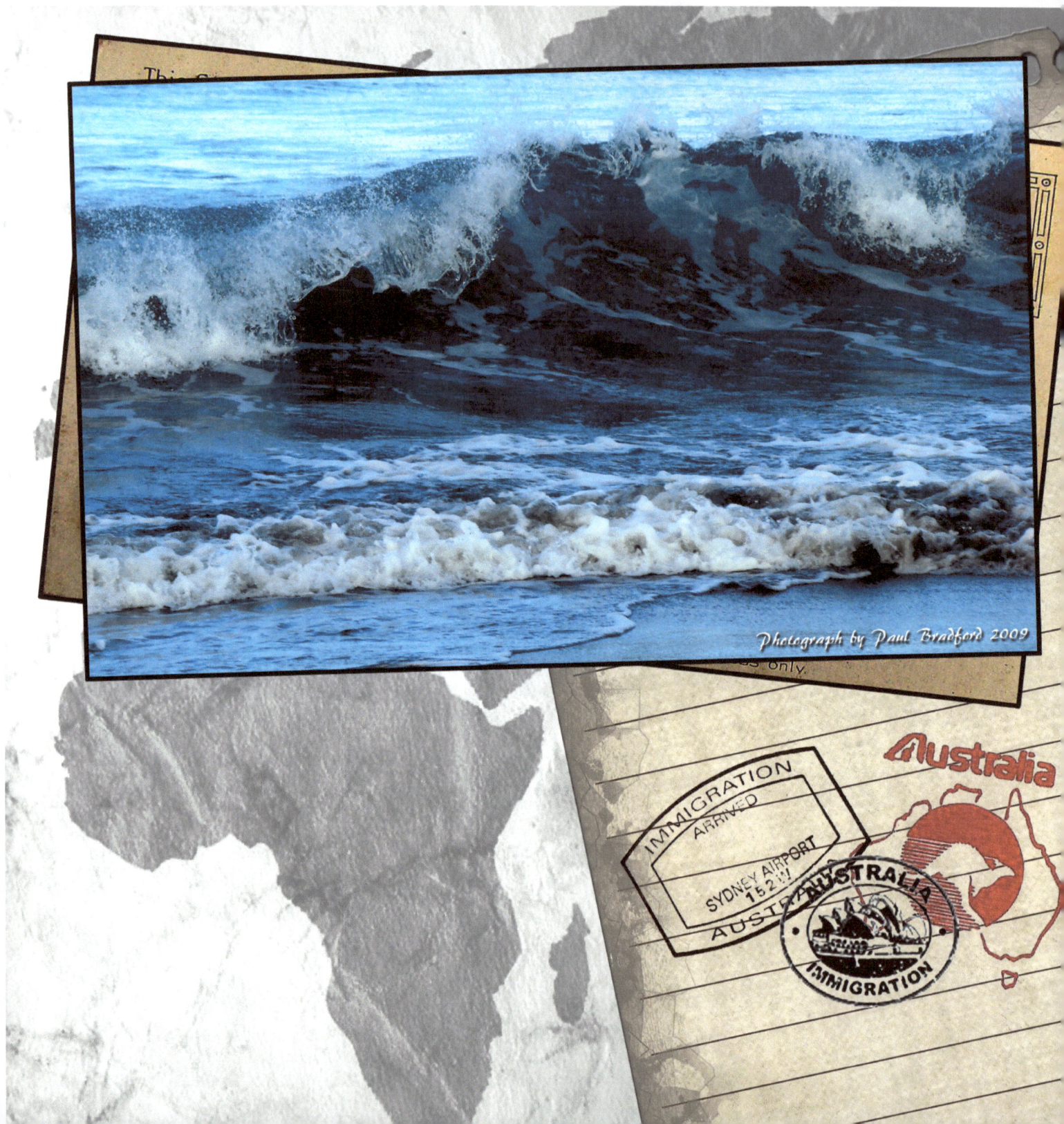

Photograph by Paul Bradford 2009

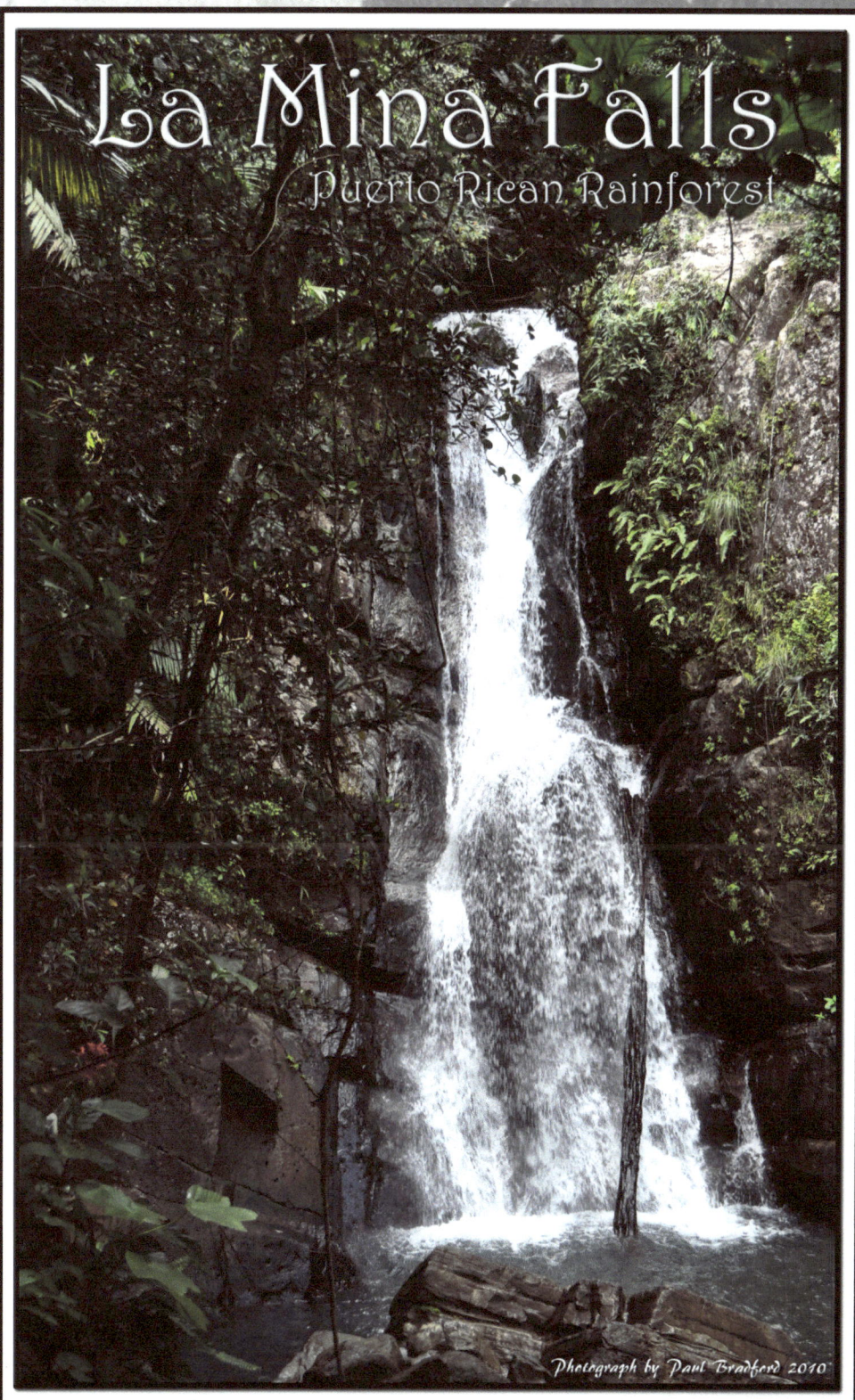

La Mina Falls
Puerto Rican Rainforest

Photograph by Paul Bradford 2010

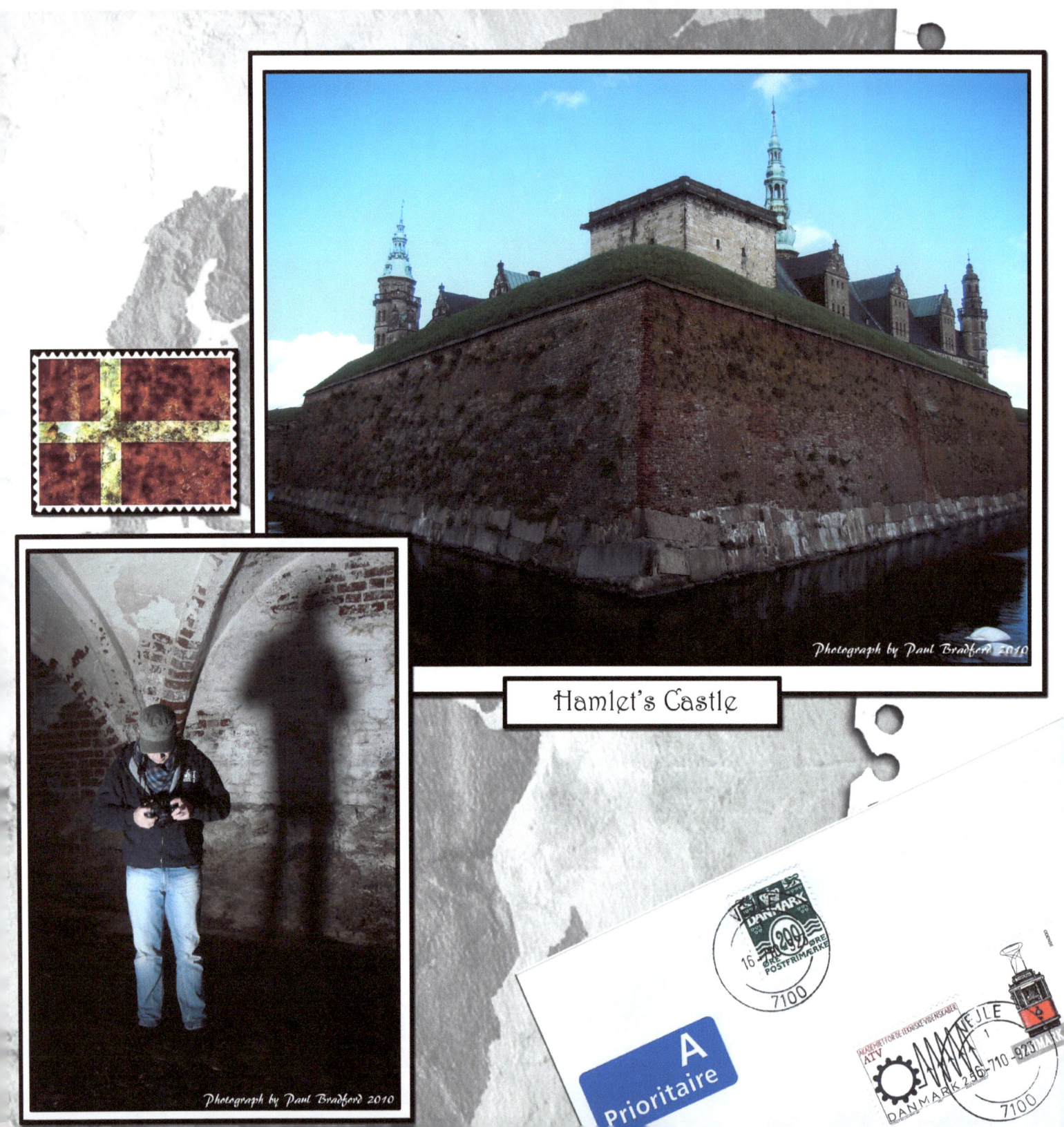

Photograph by Paul Bradford 2010

Hamlet's Castle

Photograph by Paul Bradford 2010

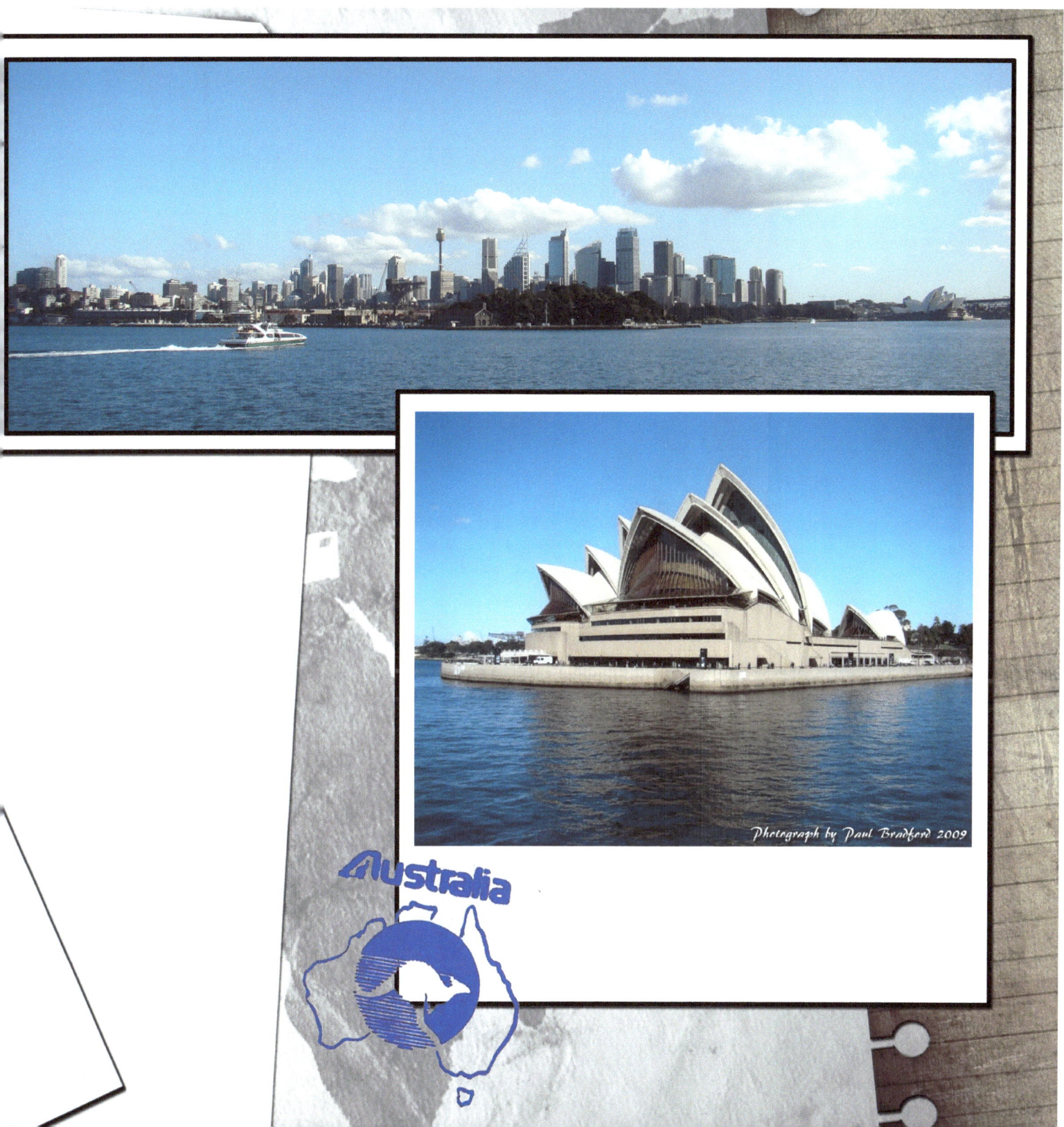

Photograph by Paul Bradford 2009

Australia

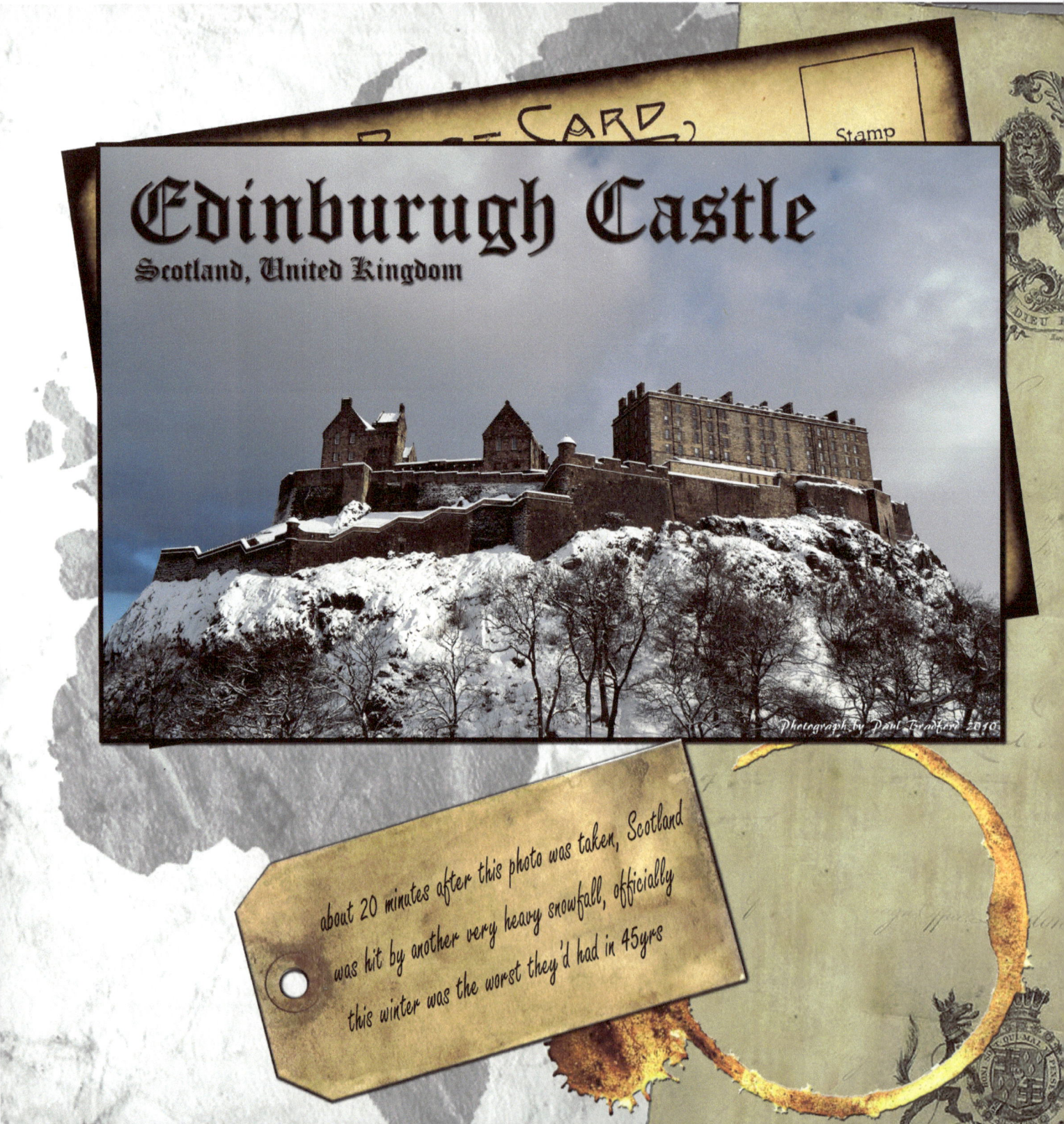

Edinburugh Castle
Scotland, United Kingdom

POST-CARD

Stamp

Photograph by Paul Bradford 2010

about 20 minutes after this photo was taken, Scotland was hit by another very heavy snowfall, officially this winter was the worst they'd had in 45yrs

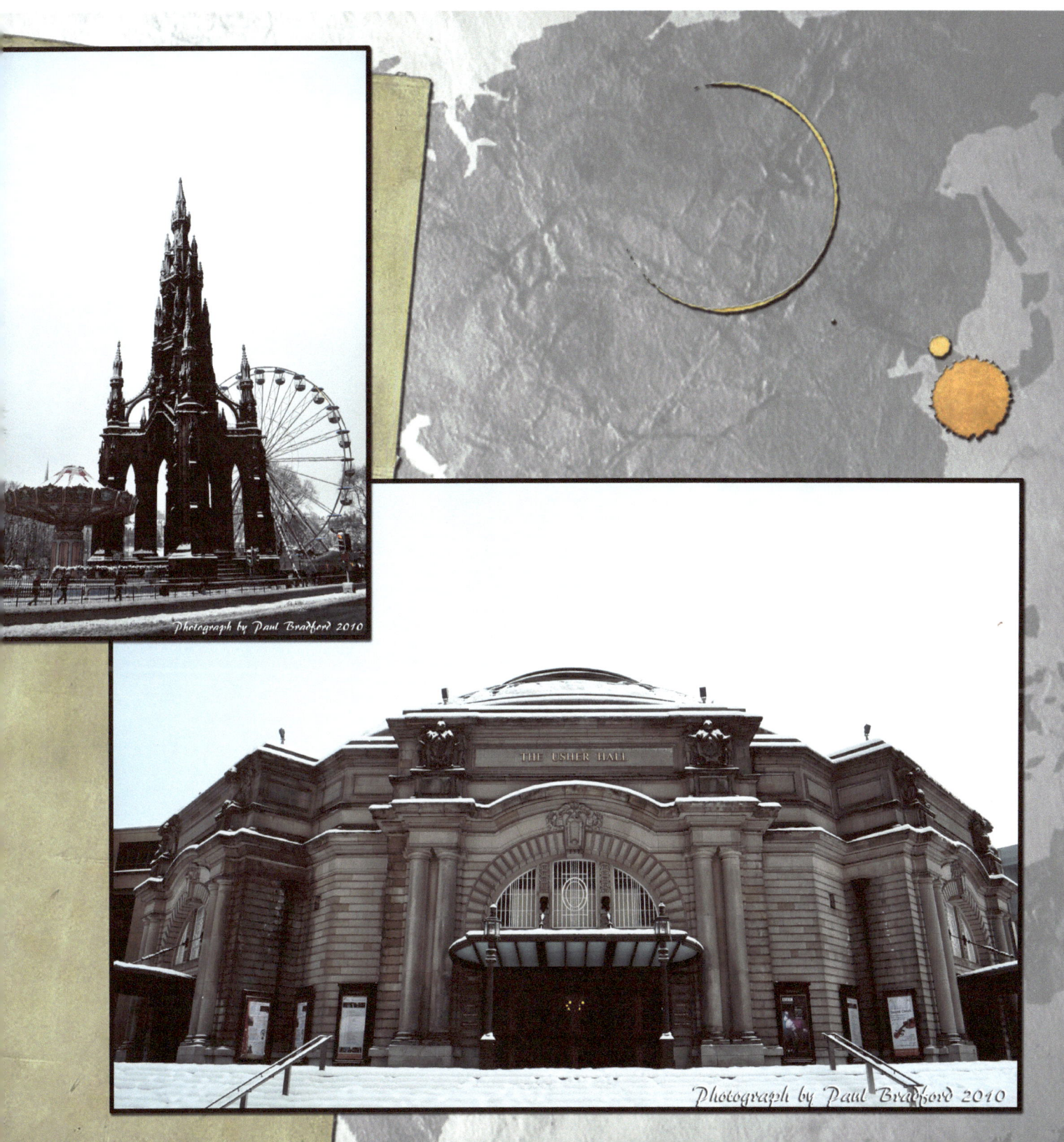

Photograph by Paul Bradford 2010

THE USHER HALL

Photograph by Paul Bradford 2010

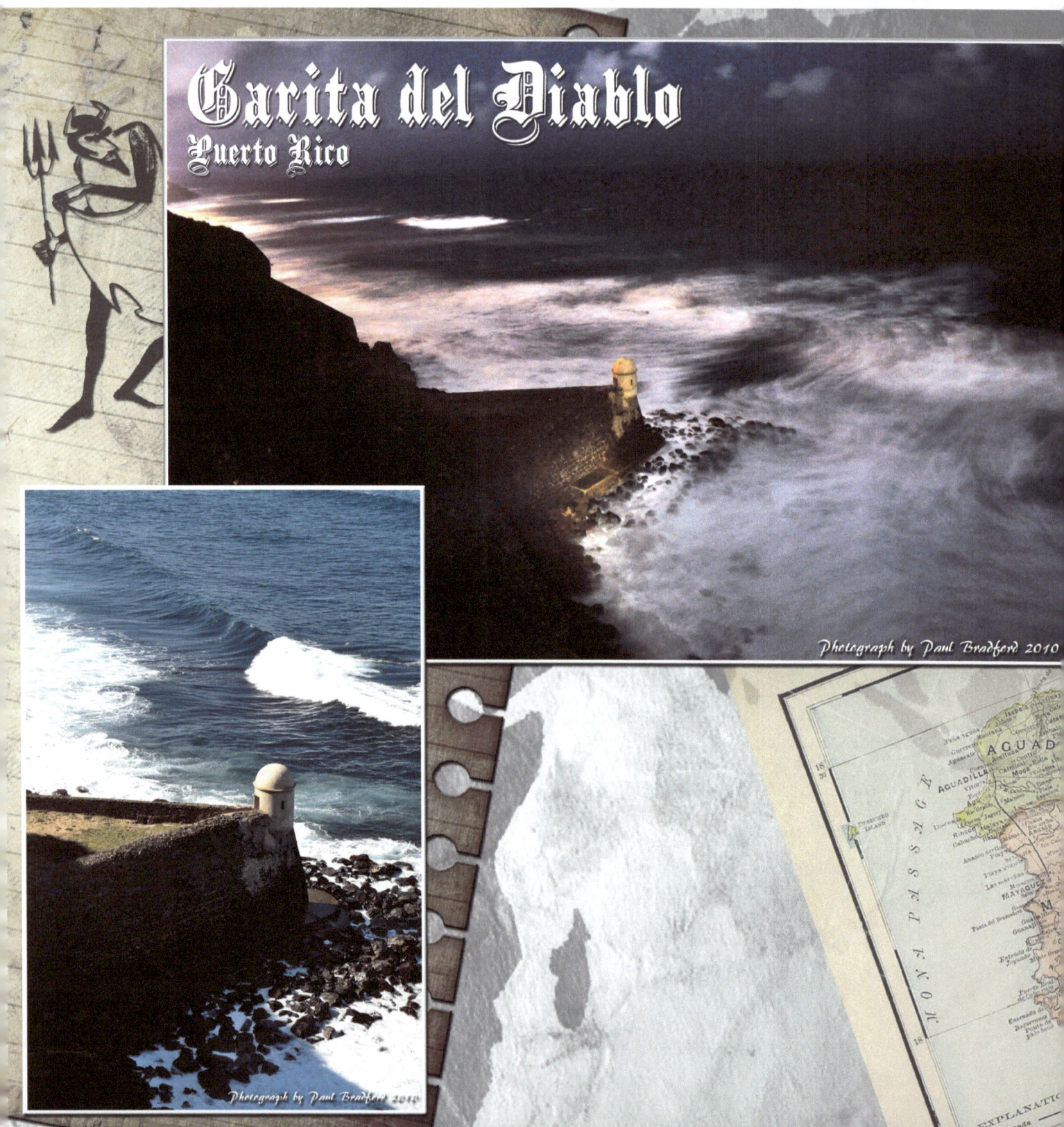

Garita del Diablo
Puerto Rico

Photograph by Paul Bradford 2010

Photograph by Paul Bradford 2010

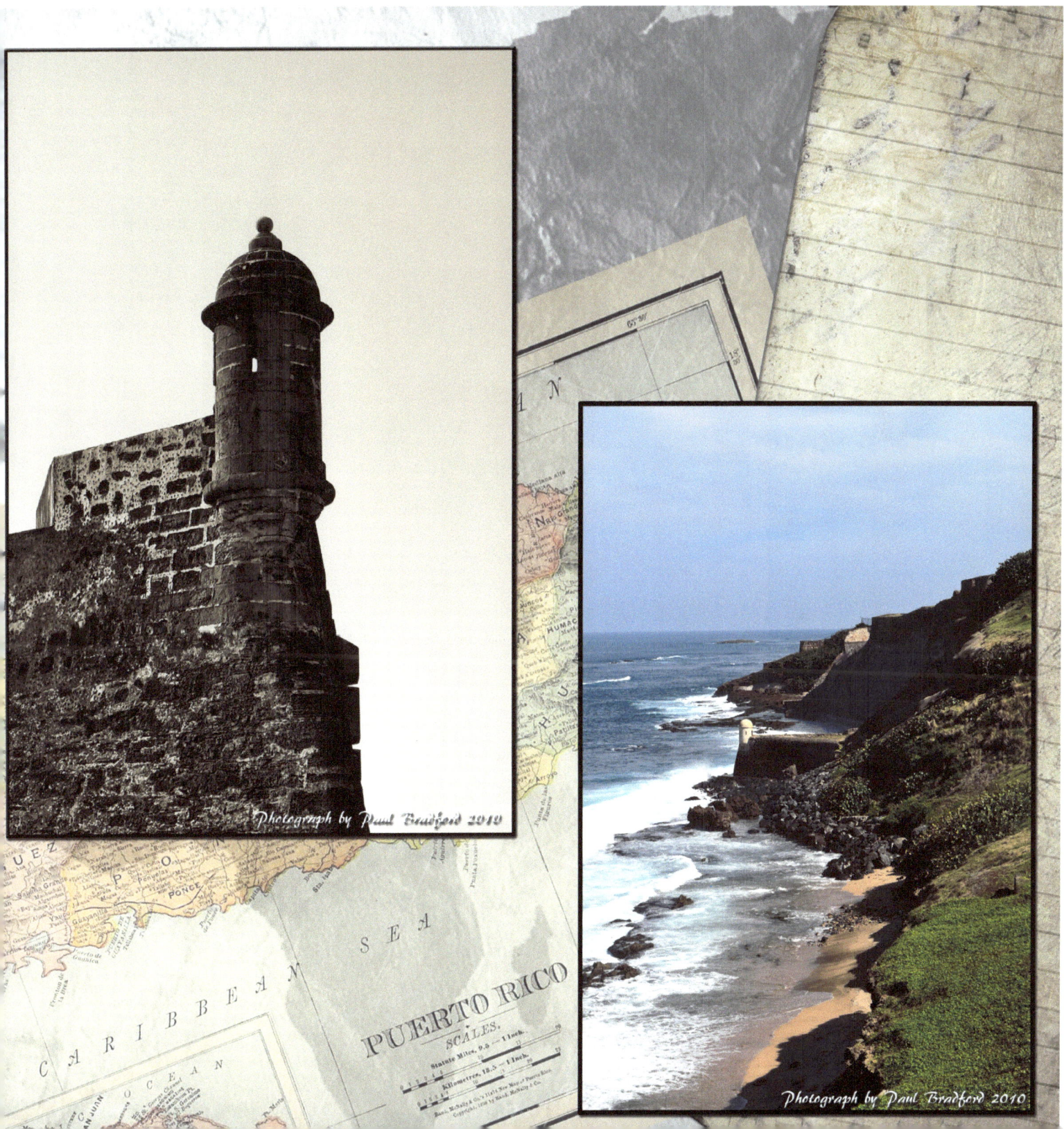

Photograph by Paul Bradford 2010

PUERTO RICO

Photograph by Paul Bradford 2010

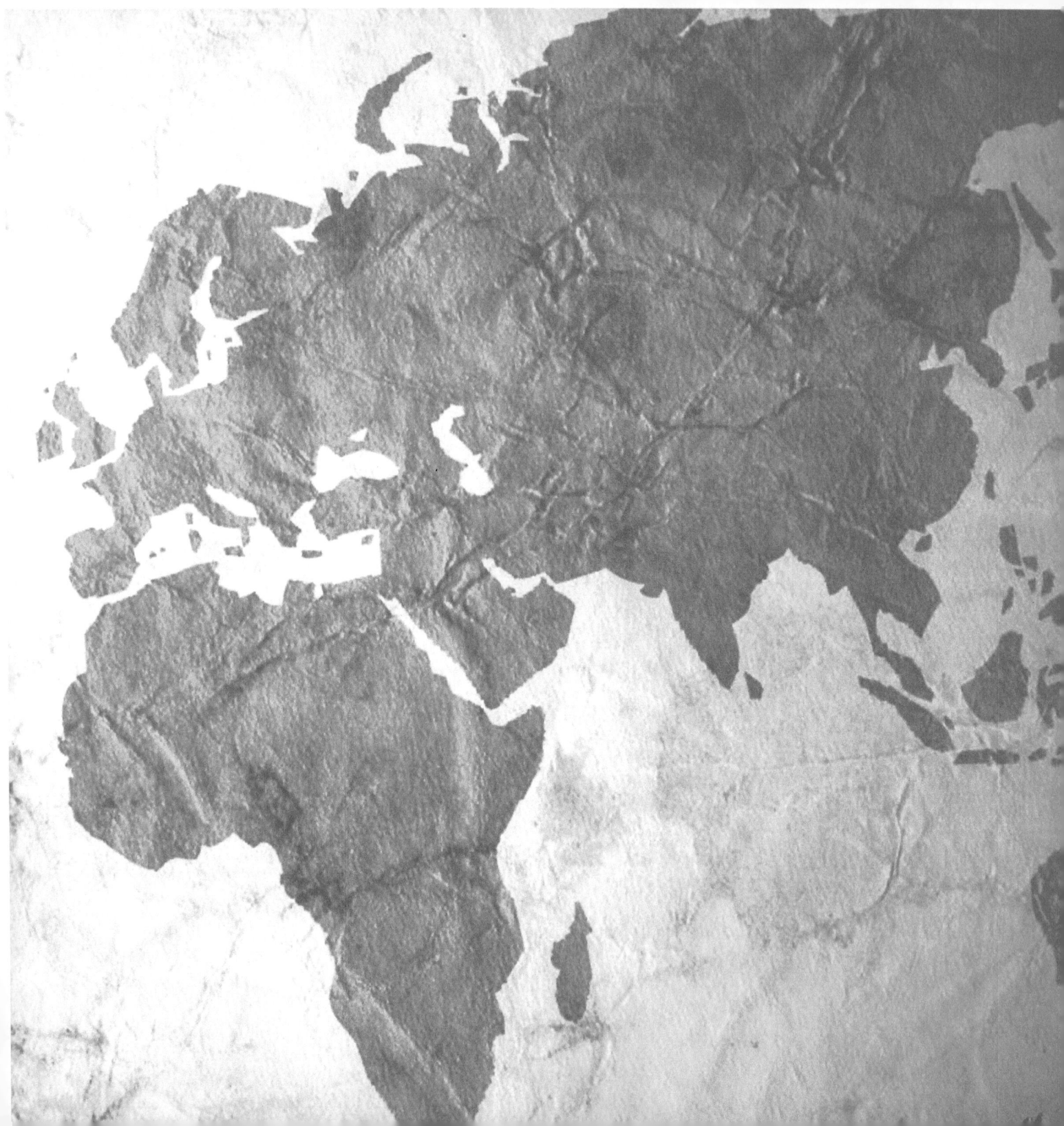

Afterword

First and foremost thank you for purchasing my first photographic book. As I've traveled the world in search of the paranormal I think it as important to take in the wonders that lay in front of us, the beauty the world has to offer and capture them in a way that potentially could last forever. I believe my photographs have a way of showing not only an image but emotion, or wonder, even something thought provoking. I hope you have enjoyed this collection and continue to share these images with others.

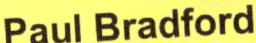

Paul Bradford

Born and raised in Britain and best known for being an international paranormal investigator on a hit television program, studied Photography and Art and Design in the UK for 4 years before becoming a professional photographer at a London Studio. He now lives in the USA with his wife and children